Do nothing from selfishness or empty conceit, but with humility of mind regard one another as more important than yourselves; do not merely look out for your own personal interests, but also for the interests of others. Have this attitude in yourselves which was also in Christ Jesus.

Phil. 2:3–5 NASB

CHRISTLIKE LEADERSHIP

Leadership that
starts with an Attitude

by
William C. Oakes

Published by
EagleWing Publishing

ISBN 1-885054-72-6
Copyright © 2003 William C. Oakes
Printed in the United States of America

CONTENTS

DEDICATION

To the followers of Jesus Christ who
will be leaders in the 21st century.

May we all prove to be worthy of our
special calling and labor chiefly
for the benefit of others.

May our attitude be to allow
Jesus Christ to live and lead
through us.

Acknowledgments

First, I thank my Lord and Savior Jesus Christ who, with a project team of only twelve members, turned Western civilization upside down.

Thanks go to my parents who raised me with love and gave me strong personal convictions. They sowed in me the belief that in order to lead, one must serve.

Thanks to my Uncle and Pastor Lloyd Oakes who practiced the Golden Rule and Servant-Leadership with more joy than anyone else I know. Pastors Bruce and Deb Sorensen gave me encouragement and insight when I needed it most.

Special thanks go to a few of my former bosses. W. Robert Reeves gave me the entrance I needed into the computer business and demonstrated many of the attitudes mentioned here. Fred Manhartsberger, Dave Lavanty, and Ken Colby each gave me priceless opportunities to experiment with these truths for myself. They were always there for me with a big safety net.

Thanks to all my teammates, coworkers, and clients over the years. Thank you for putting up with me as I experimented on you!

Thanks to Pat Keehley and Steve Medlin who challenged me to grow professionally and encouraged me to write this book.

I am deeply grateful to my children, Sarah and Ian, with whom I too often failed to practice these attitudes. I am thankful for the loving way in which they looked past my mistakes.

And most especially, and with unspeakable joy and gratitude, thanks go to my wife, Marcie, for believing in me for more than 40 years.

PREFACE

I came to leadership reluctantly. My early career aspirations were to be a writer or a college professor. Neither career would require me to lead others. Writers just write. Professors just lecture and write. Either career offered a one-way communication stream from me to whomever—and the "whomever" didn't matter too much. I wanted to write and talk at an amorphous audience more than engage with individual readers or students.

My aspirations changed, or at least matured, while I was in the Army stationed in West Germany. This was the first time I experienced leadership, someone else's intentional leadership that was focused on making all of us into leaders. Suffice it to say that I experienced horrible as well as excellent leadership, side-by-side, for three years. It taught me the virtues and benefits of becoming a good leader myself. It also inoculated me from becoming anything less.

When I returned to the states, still in the service, the Army offered me minor leadership roles at the National Security Agency. These experiences whetted my appetite for more leadership opportunities, and a desire to lead more began to grow.

When I left the Army and chose a career in computer programming, my intention was to continue to use my leadership training and experience. That led me to managing software development projects where I was responsible for accomplishing the mission, not through my own efforts alone but through the efforts of my team. It was at this point in my career, when faced with challenges far beyond my abilities, that I discovered the power and universality of the leadership principles exemplified and taught by Christ himself. It was then that I realized the power of Christlike leadership. The more I consciously employed these principles, allowing them to shape my actions and attitudes, the more successful I became and the more recognition I received.

Now I have come full circle. I am writing! But what I have written in this book speaks to individuals; it is a two-way communication stream from me to you, the reader. My intention is to connect with you and encourage you to become a more successful leader by adopting Christlike leadership attitudes at work, at home, and anywhere else.

This book is a testimony to the power of Christlike leadership—a type of leadership that simply starts with an attitude. I continue to prove to myself that this kind of leadership works. And it works for anyone who will adopt it.

Are you ready for the challenge—and the privilege—of becoming a Christlike leader?

ATTITUDE 1

FOLLOW THE GOLDEN RULE

Treat others the same way you want them to treat you.
Luke 6:31 NASB

From the time we first attend Sunday school, we are taught the single most important lesson about how to become an effective leader. "Do unto others as you would have them do unto you." Of course, it is a nonspecific idea at the time. Our parents and church teachers persuade us that it is a good idea— one that will always stand us in good stead. For many of us, the suggestion that the Golden Rule works for all situations in all circumstances takes many years to discover.

This principle of Jesus speaks of relationships between people. It says that in order to treat other people exactly how we want to be treated, we are not to seek advantage over them at their expense. It places the burden of a relationship on us. It bases the success of the outcome of any challenge on us and not on the actions of others.

How should we treat our family members, our neighbors, our friends, our acquaintances, our coworkers, our bosses? We should treat them exactly like we want them to treat us ... with respect, with compassion, with understanding, with generosity of spirit, and with forgiveness.

When we take a leadership role in putting Jesus' rule into practice, we can make a difference in our world. When we make the attitude of the Golden Rule a part of our daily lives, we will entice those from all walks of life to follow our lead, whether we are managing a complex software development project, building a space station, constructing a bridge, running a non-profit fundraiser, or coaching a girls' soccer team. Imagine the shock of those assigned to work with us in our place of business if we treat them with kindness and respect. Imagine how eager they will be to share their ideas for improvement and increased efficiency if we show how much we value their opinions and how eager we are to give them our support and recognition. Imagine the positive atmosphere that will dwell in our workplace if others follow our example and everyone practices the Golden Rule.

Lessons Learned in a Crosswalk

Many years ago, schools assigned certain students to guard the crosswalks before and after school. I was given that honor as a sixth grade student and eagerly attached a bright orange torso belt over my shirt to indicate I had the authority to stop traffic and guide students across the street. It was a position of responsibility, and I took it seriously—too seriously. I did not understand that my powers of authority had limitations. I thought I was in charge of the exact moment any student could step off the curb. I was the boss. I gloried in my first experience with power.

However, one tough-looking guy named Ralph challenged me. He had a reputation as the school bully. His father had taught him something about boxing, and he believed he was a good boxer. So did I. But the orange belt strapped across my chest empowered me. I ordered him to remain on the curb until I gave him permission to cross the street. He, of course, immediately stepped into the street and marched up to me with narrowed eyes. He told me that no one gave him orders and that I obviously needed a little lesson in order to remember that. He told me to expect that lesson during rush hour on Friday afternoon at my crosswalk.

I was afraid of Ralph. I didn't know how to fistfight or protect myself from someone's punches. I did know I could expect Ralph to follow through on his intentions. He would be at my crosswalk on Friday, and he would be on time. He was. It didn't take him long to put his fists into use. He simply walked up to me and slugged me in the right arm. Hard. Other kids were crossing the street at the time, so I tried my best to ignore Ralph. He would not be ignored. He became angrier and pummeled my arm with several more hard hits. Tears threatened to spill from my eyes from the pain and frustration.

All this time, Ralph was taunting me with names no kid wants to hear. Coward! Chicken! Sissy! Finally, I lost my temper. I took a swing at Ralph. It was a huge mistake. I hit him as hard as I could on his left arm. Ralph simply turned up the heat,

15

attacking me in other places. My retaliatory hit had only served as a catalyst for his aggression. I quickly realized that any more attempts on my part to box the boxer would end unfavorably. I tried another approach. I talked to him while he continued to punch me in the arm. No matter how many punches he made, he could not incite me to retaliate a second time.

When it was time for my duties as a crosswalk guard to end that day, I turned and walked away from the scene. Ralph followed me for a while, still punching me. I tried not to show him that I was afraid. I hoped he understood that I had no intention of fighting him. I had no idea why he had challenged my authority as a crosswalk guard, except that he was never given the honor and might have harbored resentment for those who were so honored.

The very next Monday, a most amazing thing happened. Ralph came through the crosswalk and then stayed with me until the morning bell rang. He helped me take the smaller kids safely across the street. We talked about several things but not about what had happened the previous Friday. Ralph walked into the school with me. He sought me out at recess and lunchtime, which became his pattern for the rest of the school year. Once, I slipped on the playground ice and Ralph picked me up, like a guardian angel. Another time, when a boy tried to bully me, Ralph was there again, only this time as an avenging angel. Ralph became my best friend that school year.

As we conduct our daily business, we never know if the people we come in contact with are suffering from the consequences of their previous actions, which has nothing to do with us. If their actions or words are inappropriate, insensitive, or wounding, we have the opportunity to practice Jesus' Golden Rule. As a leader, we must not be influenced by their negativity. We must listen with compassion and try to learn the reasons for their attitude, offering no equally biting comebacks. Concern and kindness can quickly deflate anger, in most situations.

When we practice the Golden Rule as a leader, we are open and honest with people. We look for their positive traits and place less focus on their negatives ones. We start them with a slate of "A" grades and wait to be shown areas where they need improvement. We provide them with second, third, and fourth chances. We offer our assistance and provide plenty of accolades for work well done. We convey the attitude that everyone makes mistakes and practice makes perfect. People follow those leaders who practice the Golden Rule and quickly adopt the same attitude.

Safety Nets

Providing an environment where we are all treated as we want to be treated means we must set up safety nets for our teammates. When we challenge our teammates to soar, to take chances, to stretch themselves, to reach their limits and go a little farther, we must also convey that we are willing and ready to catch them if they fall. We must communicate effectively that we have a safety net (a plan) in place for those moments when their risk-taking and experimentations suffer setbacks.

This sort of environment makes the workplace a fun place. People are more motivated when they are trusted. They are more energized and enthusiastic when they have a say over the things that affect their daily lives and professional decisions, and eagerly set out to prove themselves in areas they have not ventured into before. The result of this attitude is increased loyalty to the leader and to the project. When leaders empower the members of their team and protect their setbacks with safety nets, far more will be accomplished and with finer results.

Christlike leaders never assume they are infallible or that their opinions and methods for completing a project are the best. They ask for suggestions, stimulate a lively discussion of the submission, and take serious consideration of its implementation. These same leaders immediately take ownership of any mistakes they make and thank those who point them out. Such safety nets promote confidence in the leader and better cooperation among the team members. An atmosphere of acceptance and constructive criticism assures that every worthwhile project will see completion in a timely and praiseworthy way.

ATTITUDE ALIGNMENT:

Will Your Attitude Be to Follow the Golden Rule?

1. **As a leader, which if any of these roles apply to you?**
   - Pastor, coach, manager, supervisor, team leader, commanding officer, deacon, squad leader, shift leader, head cashier, mom, dad?
2. **Do you take care of others?**
   - Are you a teacher, aid, parent, doctor, nurse, mentor, big brother or sister, bus driver?
3. **Do others look to you for leadership or guidance?**
   - Would anyone call you their role model, mentor, sponsor, hero?
4. **Think about a leadership role you are in. What would change if you were to adopt this attitude of following the Golden Rule?**

ATTITUDE 2

REQUIRE AGREEMENT

... if two of you agree on earth about anything that they may ask, it shall be done for them by My Father who is in heaven. Matt. 18:19 NASB

An agreement between two people is a most powerful thing. The adage "two heads are better than one" assumes that the two heads are not only working together but are in accord with what they are doing. Christlike leaders teach their team members about being agreeable, through example. Coercion (intimidation, bullying, force) is seldom effective in the workplace. By restraining or dominating another person, a leader very quickly nullifies individual initiative.

Sometimes, when complete agreement cannot be reached, a strong leader will guide his teammates toward a compromise. Either way, the project cannot go forward if neither exists.

There are many ways for a leader to initiate either an agreement or a compromise; here are two of them.

The Old Manager Approach

The leader appoints or hires a project manager, examines all the project requirements and important dates, and makes a schedule for every project deliverable. The project manager takes the schedule to the team members responsible for actually doing the work. He points out that if they are unable to keep to the schedule, the project will fail, leaving an impression in their minds that such a failure will reflect upon them personally. The project manager declares that there is no other way to accomplish the project goal except by following the schedule formulated by the leader and by him.

If the project manager—at the leader's behest—uses his most persuasive talents and rebuts every objection made by the team members, he will eventually get their begrudging support. The leader will have accomplished the goal and fulfilled his responsibilities for the project. The team members, however, are likely to be unhappy; they will work unenthusiastically and, subconsciously, may find every way possible to prevent the schedule from being met. They may also complain, in private, about the heavy-handed ways of the leader and become clock-watchers.

The Christlike Leader Approach

The leader carefully studies the overall project requirements, important dates, and staffing resources available and comes up with a tentative schedule. He presents it to his team, taking great pains to explain that it is only a suggested schedule. He asks for their input, since they will be responsible for doing the actual work. He discusses the project's goal, the reasons for the project, the due dates for each part of the project, and perhaps the general budget. He asks for input about possible pitfalls that may affect the project's success and any solutions that may be needed in order to be prepared for them. He discusses staffing plans and other resource-related issues. He shares all available information about the project that is not considered confidential.

A leader who uses the full disclosure approach with his team members is more likely to earn their respect and cooperation. His truthfulness, humility, and attitude of fairness are well received and rewarded. The project finishes on time and to everyone's expectations. When those doing the work have input on scheduling deadlines, they progress more efficiently and with less complaining because the deadlines were theirs.

The full disclosure technique can be threatening to leaders and managers who place themselves and their reputations above everyone else's. It is especially threatening to leaders who do not practice the Golden Rule and who are not using Jesus as a role model. Encouraging agreement among every team member is vastly more powerful than coercion. Sharing information inspires cooperation and support. Workers are more likely to spend extra time on the project out of pride and the spirit of teamwork when they have a personal stake in the success of their project. Workers who are treated by their leader as having a heart and a soul and not as hollow automatons willingly follow that leader.

When a problem occurs, a good leader will accept the news with patience and understanding, listen carefully, discuss the cause with the managers and team members directly affected by the problem, and work toward a solution. A good leader will ask for and listen to the advice of all those concerned. Nothing and no one are well served by keeping the problem a secret. Whether the news is good or bad, the project team will be better motivated and better equipped to do their jobs if they are made aware of the problem and asked to participate in the solution.

In the software programming industry, it is essential for programmers of all parts of a project to be kept informed of the life of the project as a whole. If they are limited to working on only their sections of code, they will feel no sense of excitement and satisfaction when the entire project is completed. By knowing the big picture, they have a greater sense of contributing to it.

The same attitude is true in our local churches, school systems, and government. If our pastors, deacons, and board members are secretive about their discussions and concerns, members of the congregation are likely to get caught up in rumors and misinformation. If the school superintendent and principals set rules and agendas without the input of the teachers, the students may be the ones to suffer the consequences. Unhappy teachers cannot teach effectively. When members of a team feel appreciated and valued, they are more enthusiastic about their roles. Leaders earn respect by showing respect for those in their charge.

When a project team has two classes of citizens—the leader and manager in one class and the workers in the other—no one can enjoy the benefits of agreement. There is power in agreement, and agreement usually involves compromise. Being upfront with our teammates and keeping them in the loop regarding the needs of the project encourages cooperation. We are all alike in our need for appreciation. We are all alike in wanting to see a project completed as envisioned and to the satisfaction of those who put us in charge

There is always the possibility that a project simply can't be completed as originally envisioned. Some projects are so ambitious, expectations are set so high, and goals are so "out there" that no one can pull it off. In these cases, it is important for leaders to inform both the client and the team members of potential problems. The sooner they know this, the less stress and frustration will likely occur to further complicate the issue. Effective leaders own up to problems. Christlike leaders are honest. Problems are a given when projects depend on less than perfect human beings, technology, and weather conditions.

Put Your Cards on the Table

I worked on a software development project that called for a system of approximately 140 software modules or programs that were to be designed, built, and tested in a six-month timeframe. After discussing it with the project leader and my managers, I received the staffing I deemed necessary to accomplish the project. I examined the project, established the guidelines I thought necessary for its success, and shared these with my project team, soliciting their schedule dates for each task and deliverable.

However, it quickly became apparent that my strategic study of the project lacked depth and content. There were more modules than originally identified—many more. Almost three times as many! I immediately shared these discrepancies with the client and my team. I was embarrassed to do so, of course, because the problem was with my inexact planning. There were extenuating circumstances, however, and the client was aware of them. The client was convinced I had done the best job anyone could have done under these circumstances.

Unfortunately, the error in planning meant that the members of my team had even more work to accomplish than originally designed. The timeframes for the project remained the same. In order to accomplish the additional work, we needed to exert more effort, get more people, or both. I apologized to the team members for the error in judgment, explained how it had happened, and told them that as long as they each gave me their very best efforts, I would make sure they were individually successful. I assured them that I alone would take any heat from the client. In short, I laid all the cards on the table, asking them to save the project for the company.

All the "cards on the table" were picked up ... voluntarily. Every new programming module was added to someone's schedule. People volunteered to help each other if they got ahead on their own work. Morale remained high, and the motivation and enthusiasm of each participant became contagious. Instead of writing 140 modules in six months, my team was able to write more than 300 modules. That was not good enough. We needed fifty more modules to complete the system. We missed the deadline and the target of delivering a workable system. Despite this setback, my team and I could still consider the project a success.

Client Agreement

We were a success because we had shared the day-to-day problems and successes of the project with each other and with our client. We held nothing back from them. Every Tuesday, we presented an accurate picture of the project, both in person and in writing.

How did we pull this project out of its death spiral? By continually sharing information and soliciting support from the client and from each other, we were able to achieve mutual accountability for the problems. We joined forces—for rather than against each other. I could have gone to the client and waved the contract, giving them only what we had originally planned on giving them. I could have gone to my project team and mandated that they work harder, smarter, and longer, not admitting my failures. The result would have been a failed project and a nonworking system. Coercion would have worsened the project's problems. My team members would not have followed my leadership.

Agreement Is Powerful

The finished project pleased the client and my company's leaders. The client continued to do business with us and allowed us to use them as a reference. Gaining agreement with clients can be more difficult than with team members, but it is even more important. Clients are the ultimate and final judge of success as a project leader. They are the ones who really count. They are always right. They are the only reason for our existence as a project leader. Without them, there are no projects.

What if we are placed in charge of the church building fund instead of a software project? What if we grossly underestimate the cost of materials for the new building? How will we handle such a problem? The only way for Christian leaders to handle any problem is with honesty and humility. We admit the mistake in our numbers and come to a new agreement based on the new estimates.

ATTITUDE ALIGNMENT:

Will Your Attitude Be to Require Agreement?

1. **Do you share your life with people with whom you need to gain agreement?**
   - With your spouse? Your children? Your parents and in-laws? Your siblings? Other close relatives? Your friends? Your hunting and fishing buddies?
2. **Do you worship with people with whom you need to gain agreement?**
   - With the pastor? The church staff? The board members, elders, and deacons? The church volunteers?
3. **Do you work with people with whom you need to gain agreement?**
   - With the boss? Peers and co-workers? Teammates? Your direct staff? Your administrative support personnel? What about people in HR, accounting and finance, engineering, marketing, customer support, sales? Your building contractor?
4. **Are you willing to adopt this attitude? It will mean not just desiring agreement but truly working for it and requiring it of yourself and others. What situation faces you today that needs a greater degree of agreement?**

ATTITUDE 3

Sow Only Good Seed

For you will render to a man according to his work.
Psalm 62:12 ESV

... for whatever one sows, that will he also reap.
Gal. 6:7 ESV

The law of sowing and reaping is perhaps the most powerful of the universal laws of creation. Contained within it is the most basic truth: everything comes from something else. A thing must change in some way—great or small—in order for a new thing to come into being. The reverse perspective is equally true. If anything has changed, we can be sure it changed because something else caused it to do so.

Change is inevitable, manageable, and preferable to the alternative. A good project team is on the constant lookout for change—changes to requirements, technology used, skill mix of personnel, funding arrangements, client's expectations. Uncontrolled change is the death of a project, but change in and of itself is not to be feared. Sometimes things happen that we wish hadn't, and other times things happen because we cause them. We mustn't fear change or avoid it. Rather, we must embrace it as being inevitable.

The sign of a good project is one that effectively handles change, establishes procedures to make the changes manageable, and welcomes the change when it is clearly better than the status quo.

Sow Expecting to Reap

The law of sowing and reaping permeates every aspect of project management, church leadership, coaching, teaching ... and even parenting. When we treat others—even our children—as we would like to be treated, we are planting the seeds of that attitude in them. When we deal with others in an honest, straightforward manner, we are planting the seeds of that attitude in them. We can and should expect to reap the same attitudes.

Some change is generated externally; it comes upon us. Other change is self-generated. We wish to improve our skills in a certain area, conquer a new technology or skill, learn more about a subject, put into practice a newly found talent. This is accomplished through a sowing and reaping process. If we wish to learn more about financial budgeting, software testing, or the customs of the Bible, or if we want to take on additional responsibilities at work, at church, or at the football stadium, we start with seeds. We plant small seeds that we know will someday reap for us the harvest we want. We read a number of books on the subject, we sign up for a college class, we volunteer to help out more, or we offer to take a turn at coaching or whatever. A seed-sowing attitude will see us planting good seeds daily into our lives and the lives of those around us.

Reaping the Unexpected

The real challenge comes when we as leaders are caught unaware by a serious change to our project. Maybe we planted the seeds of change unknowingly. Maybe we purposely planted the seeds and simply hoped we could get away with it this one time because we wanted the project. Maybe someone else screwed up. Maybe our client threw us a sudden curve, demanding new and expanded functionality out of the system. Maybe the building contractor grossly underestimated the cost of materials, labor, or charges due to weather delays. It doesn't make any difference what the predicament is, the important thing is how we are going to deal with it using our Christian principles.

We must be bold and take the initiative. We are called to leadership because others have faith in us and believe we can show the way. We must show that we are willing to take the risk of being completely honest and open about our need for support. We must understand that we can only control our own behavior and reactions. We cannot control anyone else's.

Projects do not get into trouble because they are properly managed. They get into trouble because something is out of whack, something is wrong, something was overlooked, or something has changed. The best medicine for this situation is for us to admit where the problems and shortcomings are, come up with a plan to correct them, and then move on.

Sometimes, though, the unexpected happens and deadlines are shortened. Leaders are the first to adopt and demonstrate that urgency. When team members need to work extra hard and for longer hours, the leader must also come in earlier, leave later, and work weekends.

When Jesus of Nazareth was about to be crucified, He said He would gladly go to the cross because of the glory it would bring afterward. When He carried out such a selfless act, the seeds of Christianity were sown. Any sacrifices we make as the leader of a project (our leisure time, an expected bonus, a formerly scheduled vacation, having everything done our way) will often produce more in the harvesting of goodwill and loyalty from our team members. There is no reprieve from the harvest. It must be brought in. The good news is that we can learn from our mistakes and plant fewer bad seeds, starting today.

ATTITUDE ALIGNMENT:

Will our Attitude Be to Sow Only Good Seed?

1. **Do you need to improve your own personal or professional skills and performance?**
    - Through more college or other training? More opportunities for life experiences? More quiet reflection on what has already happened?

2. **Do you need to improve the quality, performance, or professionalism of the team?**
    - Through more team or individual training? More team-building activities? More of your personal time and attention?

3. **Do you need to improve a relationship?**
    - With your spouse? A teammate? A member of the church? The parent of a child that you teach or coach? An unhappy business client? Your boss?

4. **Can you identify some bad seed that you are reaping today? What good seed can you start sowing instead? Don't forget to stop sowing the bad seed!**

ATTITUDE 4

BE A SERVANT-LEADER

But the greatest among you shall be your servant. Whoever exalts himself shall be humbled; and whoever humbles himself shall be exalted.
Matt. 23:11,12 NASB

Jesus washed the feet of his disciples as a lesson in humility. He said that as His disciples, they must learn to serve those who serve Him in a like manner. Gandhi was also a servant-leader. He devoted his life to being an example of peace and charity in India. There are other men and women throughout history who have demonstrated this attitude: biblical leaders such as Abraham, Moses, Ruth, and Saul of Tarsus; American and religious leaders such as George Washington, Abraham Lincoln, Martin Luther King, Jr., Billy Graham, Pope John Paul II, and Mother Teresa. As we work toward acquiring the traits of Jesus in order to lead with honor, we can learn from reading about the service of these others, as well. They exhibited many of the same qualities. Each wanted to serve as leaders of the people, and they accomplished great things, often at their own expense.

While none of them were perfect, each was a servant-leader worthy of emulation.

The Reluctant Sergeant

I spent eleven years in the U.S. Army as a linguist. I enlisted and eventually attained the rank of staff sergeant before leaving the service. I say "eventually" because I could have reached that rank much sooner if I had been willing to accept two recommendations for promotion when they were first offered to me. I was young and full of principles and ideals. I had a low opinion of most noncommissioned officers (NCOs), commonly known as sergeants. I labeled them as dictatorial, demanding, and uncaring egomaniacs. All of them. A promotion in rank meant that I, too, would become an NCO.

During an extended field training exercise in what was then West Germany, it suddenly dawned on me that there were good NCOs and bad NCOs. The good NCOs protected their troops and looked out for their safety and welfare. These NCOs had the admiration and respect of their soldiers. On the other hand, the bad NCOs seemed to be surrounded by troublesome, poorly motivated soldiers.

I watched as soldiers from one group were transferred to the other. In short order, their behavior changed; the soldiers conformed to the group norm. Those who arrived with negative attitudes and slovenly behavior quickly took on the attitude of the good NCO to whom they were assigned. Those soldiers who once had been highly motivated quickly became jaded and detached under the leadership of a bad NCO. I experienced the change myself when I was reassigned from one squad leader to another. I soon reflected my squad leader's attitudes. Although my revelation came slowly, I came to realize the best way to enjoy my tour of duty was to become one of the good NCOs. Then I could make my life as well as my team members' lives more rewarding. I couldn't change the whole world, but I could change one small piece of it. One by one, I accepted my promotions, which came in quick succession.

Successful leadership starts with the leader's attitude about his team and its mission. A committed, energetic, enthusiastic, and inspiring leader is more likely to have a cooperative, hardworking, and victorious team. Such leaders know they are not infallible. They know they are responsible to and for everyone assigned to them. Leaders are servants who care about their team members.

The Glory of Servant-Leadership

There is a movie titled *Glory* that deals with the first black regiment of the Civil War, led by a young, privileged Northern white officer. This young leader was firm yet fair. He was willing to sacrifice his own pleasure for the good of the unit. He was willing to charge at the head of the column into enemy guns. He served through example by showing them the value of selflessness, bravery, and high principles. Each member in the regiment was responsible to only one man—the commanding officer—but he was responsible to all of them.

Unfortunately, the picture we have of a modern leader is someone who sits in his office, often behind closed doors, handing out decrees to subordinate managers who, in turn, hand them to the operating members of the team. This type of leader is more in the mold of a military dictator who rules by intimidation and fear. If we examine his business, we are likely to find poor morale, little enthusiasm, a high incidence of illness, and considerable turnover in personnel. This is the case unless, of course, one of *his* managers takes it upon himself to be a servant-leader. Too many of our team and group leaders emulate their authoritarian, old-school bosses, thinking it is the path to their success. The sign of success, they think, is to keep people in reverential fear of them.

Even in the military, where everyone is conscious of rank, the military salute is considered a sign of mutual respect, not a sign of servitude. When a sergeant salutes his lieutenant or company commander, he shows respect for them and their office. When they return the salute, they show their respect for the sergeant as a person and as a soldier.

Most of us choose to emulate leaders of compassion and perspective who call us by our name, who know of and respect our personal goals, and who willingly discuss them and suggest ways to pursue and excel in them. We are drawn to leaders who will stand up for us when we make a mistake and who provide a safety net so we can try new things and not fear failure.

We willingly give glory (honor, admiration, loyalty) to servant-leaders.

The Reward of Servant-Leadership

The movie *Spartacus* has a scene near the end where the victorious Roman military officers order the leader, Spartacus, to step forward. When no one immediately obeys, they offer a bargain. The soldier in the defeated slave army who will identify Spartacus and turn him over for execution will save himself from being crucified. Spartacus is the first to step forward and identify himself. Because of his bravery and selflessness, every other man in the company steps forward to argue that he is the real Spartacus.

Spartacus felt a mixture of unspeakable pride and humility at that moment. His project team showed him loyalty and devotion. How had he achieved such respect? Through heavy-handed tactics? Through fear and intimidation? Through the promise of stock options and bonuses? Through micromanagement? Through the keeping of secrets? By assuming the worst of his men, all of whom were slaves and convicts?

He reaped the rewards of loyalty and respect by accepting responsibility for his troops, by leading them in battle, by being willing to die with them and for them, by placing their needs above his own, and by earning their trust and admiration through his enthusiasm for completing their mission.

ATTITUDE ALIGNMENT:

Will Your Attitude Be to Become a Servant-Leader?

1. **Do you have trouble attracting people to work on your projects?**
   - How do you come across to people when they first meet you? Do you seem too busy to bother with them? Do they feel safe working with you?

2. **Do you have trouble keeping people working on your projects?**
   - What is your management style? Are you demanding? Are you protective, another word for secretive and privileged? Are you solicitous of others' ideas? Do you trust others to do as good a job as you can?

3. **Do you have trouble attracting friends and keeping them?**
   - Are you open with people? Do people want to be around you? Do you make them feel more important than yourself? Are you genuine?

4. **Name three things that are needed in someone's life, or in your team's life, that you believe are beneath you to perform or provide? Would Christ feel that way? Are you willing to adopt His attitude toward these things?**

ATTITUDE 5

DELEGATE AND EMPOWER

*Furthermore, you shall select out of all the people able men
who fear God, men of truth, those who hate dishonest gain;
and you shall place these over them, as leaders of thousands, of
hundreds, of fifties and of tens.
If you do this thing and God so commands you, then you
will be able to endure, and all these people also will go to their
place in peace.*
Exod. 18:21, 23 NASB

Moses was advised by his father-in-law Jethro to delegate
and empower others or his goal would likely fail. Moses was a
servant at heart. Unfortunately, he became trapped by his own
servanthood. He could not possibly serve the multitude of the
Hebrew nation without assistance. Even though his heart was
in the right place, his attitude precluded him from serving
effectively as the Exodus project manager. He could not know
everything or be attentive to every detail that required action.

To better serve his God and the people of Israel, Moses
needed to delegate some of his authority. He had to impose

upon others part of the burden he had volunteered to shoulder alone. It was probably not an easy thing for him to do. Leaders have more control over the outcome if they retain management of the entire project. Moses understood that although he would need to allow others to share in the fulfillment of their goals, he would still hold the responsibility for the success of the venture. Unfortunately, Moses appointed managers who did not share his vision, and when chaos ensued and the Hebrews lost focus on the reason for their journey, God held Moses accountable for their despicable behavior and disobedience.

It is within our right as the leader of a project to delegate to others the power to decide and act, but the responsibility for the final result is still ours. We remain the ultimate authority and must carefully oversee and guide our project managers so they keep their focus on that end result.

Finding the Best Qualified Leaders

Most of us are interested in career advancement. There are usually two tracks we can follow: technical or managerial. Through the setting of personal and professional goals, we should get to know who on our team wishes to move along the management track.

There are generally more potential managers than management positions, and we will likely have a long list of people who want to be team leaders. We must first ascertain how many team leaders we need. This will influence how large the team is, how many team locations there are, how complex the work is, and so forth.

Next, we must consider our own availability and capability. Delegating authority to team leaders requires that we become even more involved in their career and personal development goals and in how they influence those under their direction. We run the risk of placing people in positions where they could undermine the morale or effectiveness of the entire project team. All we have accomplished in the way of improving team morale, enthusiasm, and urgency can be destroyed by placing the wrong person in a leadership role or by not spending enough time supervising that new leader.

It is important, then, that we spend time with team leaders, old and new. They need guidance not only in how to lead effectively but also in how to lead within the project or organization. They must be assured that we will give them great latitude in how to best accomplish their role in the whole, but that we also take our ultimate responsibilities seriously.

We will be there to help out and discuss problems and progress, but there will be limits. We will provide them with a safety net at all times so long as they treat their team members properly and strive to achieve the project's goals in an efficient and timely manner. Delegating authority does not mean less work for us, only work of a different nature.

Our intention is not to create clones of ourselves. Everyone is different and sees the same forest through different eyes. That is a good thing. How a task is accomplished is not as important as whether it is done in accordance with some set standards or attitudes.

Gaining the Acceptance of Team Members

Kate was an inexperienced team leader who had some difficulty with one of her team members who was more technically qualified and experienced and chose to take out her frustrations on her leader. Kate came to me and asked how she should handle the situation.

I told Kate that I choose to lead by example, that I was not a know-it-all and made no claims of having the ability to do everything well. I tried to practice the Golden Rule. However, my way may not be her way. She needed to find her own style and way of dealing with the issue while maintaining the positive and admirable attitudes of a leader—patience, understanding, compassion, and fairness.

Left unspoken, of course, was the fact that if she could not overcome this problem, she may not be the team leader much longer. Since I was responsible for the completion of the project and ultimately for the contentment of all my team members, no single person—team leader or not—was more important than the others. Therefore, I had my eye on Kate and hoped for a satisfactory outcome.

Kate took my advice, adopted the proper attitude, and acted in accordance with her own style and personality. I would have held a serious conference in my office, but Kate, a more social person, spoke with the disgruntled team member in a more casual after-work environment, poking fun at herself and easing the tense situation with good humor. The final outcome was that the two worked very well together. Kate showed her teammate that she excelled as a team leader because she was proficient and wise in dealing with difficult clients, understanding contractual limitations, planning schedules in detail, and knowing her own limitations and when to call for help. Kate admitted to the team member that she was deficient in technical prowess. The disgruntled teammate appreciated her honesty and confidence and volunteered her assistance when technical issues were involved. She also came to appreciate Kate's valuable organizational and people skills. Once all the cards were on the table, all parties came to an agreement on the situation.

Respect Must Be Earned

A very capable young man on my team had an intense drive to get into management. His technical skills were as good as anyone's on the team, and he had as much experience as his teammates in software development. However, he was completely dismissed by the others as being ineffective. They didn't like working with him. I surmised that at least some of the problem was simply a personality clash.

Under these circumstances, I certainly could not put the young man in charge of a team. On the one hand, I believed he was talented and could be a help to others on the project; on the other hand, if they weren't willing to work with him, the project as a whole would likely not see completion.

As leader of the project, I needed to select project managers who were the best qualified and who wanted to challenge themselves for career advancement. I had to trust my judgment and be fair to the individuals. In this particular situation, I needed to weigh the opinions of others while understanding their needs, motivations, and prior personal experiences. I certainly couldn't put the entire team in a difficult situation simply for the benefit of one person.

I placed the young man in charge of the technical configuration of our development environment and gave him a small area of the project to work on more or less by himself. Since the team's problem was one of perception more than reality in that the members perceived their cohort as someone not worthy of their respect, I established an environment where I could prove he was worthy. I showed my respect for the man. In his capacity as the configuration manager, the members had to go to him for answers and assistance on configuration matters. I made it a point to thank him in open meetings for his having accomplished a task in a short time, and so forth.

Giving this young man a small piece of the project to work on by himself allowed him an opportunity to understand the analysis procedure the rest of the project team was going through and also demonstrate to the others that he was, indeed, capable. The project benefited from his participation, and he delivered the areas he was responsible for on time with good quality.

Shepherds, Not Cowboys

Leaders must often assume the role of mentor. While it is almost always rewarding, it can be very time consuming. Sometimes, those who want very much to take on the leader's responsibilities are not qualified. Some are more interested in simply assuming the role to add it to their résumés. Some are only interested in the prestige or the power the role may bring them. Some want respect by decree. Some want what they believe is an easier job. Some want to be seen as part of the inner circle. Some want more money. Such people can be referred to as cowboys—those who are eager to herd the cattle along to the slaughter house so they can collect their money and go off to spend it.

A few others genuinely want to contribute to the project by guiding others through the process. They enjoy challenges and look for opportunities to learn more. They want to try out new ideas in a protected environment where they can make mistakes and learn from them. They enjoy working with others, and team spirit is important to them. They have no interest in capturing all the credit for a job well done but are philanthropic by nature. They have a burning desire to serve to the best of their ability. They can be likened to shepherds, guiding their flock to good pasture and clean water in safety and with careful tending.

Both types of people are ambitious, and that is a requirement.

The analogy of the cattle driver and sheep herder is a good one because there are significant differences between the two. It is no coincidence that the Bible talks about people as being like sheep and not cows. Sheep are timid by nature and need tending. They stay close together and are not very adventurous. They cannot defend themselves against challenges from nature.

They need the shepherd. Often, members of a team project are like this. They need the wisdom and tending from an effective and caring leader who can guide them through the tasks required to achieve the goal. They need a leader who offers encouragement when needed and praise when earned. They need a leader who is like a shepherd. Those who aspire to become leaders will find no better mentor than Jesus Christ, the Good Shepherd.

Succession Planning

A most important feature of proper delegation is that it facilitates effective succession planning. Succession planning is the intentional identification of our successor and the enabling of that person to do our job, should the need arise.

Yet, succession planning is virtually every team member's job. Practicing succession planning on the lowest skilled positions is not necessary, but what about our team leads? What if we were to suddenly lose our senior programmers, our architects, or our administrators? Bad things happen to everyone. Terrible calamities can befall people, like getting hit by a bus while crossing the street. A team member may simply decide to take a different job. In any case, if we haven't been doing our succession planning, we're going to endanger the project schedule, at a minimum.

Bad things happen to good people and to good projects. Projects are made up of people, and when any one of them becomes unavailable for any reason, the project will suffer. The only way to combat this highly volatile risk is by exercising proper succession planning, and that means being willing to delegate and empower others. It is our project's only means of survival for the long term.

What did Jesus do? He worked in his ministry on earth for less than four years. During that time, He delegated much of His project to His twelve disciples, empowering them with enough authority to be successful at their assigned tasks, even in His earthly absence.

ATTITUDE ALIGNMENT:

Will Your Attitude Be to Delegate and Empower?

1. **If someone stopped fulfilling his or her role, suddenly and unexpectedly, what would happen?**
   - Would the project or team suffer? Would your church? Would your little brother or sister? Would the team you coach?

2. **If you never took a day off, worked every weekend, never delegated anything, wouldn't that be a good thing, a sacrificial thing, to do?**
   - How could it cause harm to anyone else's career? How could it put the project in jeopardy?

3. **If you allowed others to do part of your job with full authority, wouldn't that mean you are expendable?**
   - Do you fear that your boss might get rid of you? Isn't your job to lead and manage, not to let others do it? Leaders don't delegate, do they?

ATTITUDE 6

WRITE EVERYTHING DOWN

*Write the vision; make it plain on tablets,
so he may run who reads it.*
Hab. 2:2 ESV
*Then the Lord said to Moses, "Write down these words,
for in accordance with these words I have made a covenant
with you and with Israel."*
Exod. 34:27 NASB

We have all played the party game "Telephone" where a short story is whispered into one person's ear. That person, in turn, whispers the story into the next person's ear, and so on around the room. The fun occurs when we listen to the story as the last person heard it. The more people involved in spreading the story, the more outlandish the tale becomes.

Projects are a lot like this party game. One bit of information is spread among the various groups and individuals. Seldom does the whole truth and only the truth get disseminated.

While there is no way to stop rumors and no real reason to try, it is important to get the right information out to all of our project people.

The question is, *How?*

Not Only in the Business World

Before we get into some very practical ways to solve this ever present problem in the business world, we need to understand that this attitude is just as important in the nonbusiness world. Putting things in writing, particularly via status reports, is a worthwhile practice for every project, even for a girls' soccer team or a local church rummage sale. While this does not guarantee to stop rumors and gossiping, at least some of the truth will be officially disseminated to offset the idle chatter and unhelpful speculation.

The Importance of Sharing

Too many pastors believe their congregations don't need to know about (or wouldn't be interested in knowing about) the status of the church. As leaders of their church congregations, they fail to serve effectively when they don't share information with their people on a regular basis. They treat their members like visitors and guests rather than the teammates they truly are—teammates in the cause of Christ, sharing a vision for their community.

What happened this week in the life of the church? How many people got involved in various types of ministries? How were the church funds and staff utilized? What new opportunities or challenges arose during the course of the week? How can the church use the talents and knowledge of its team members better? How can team members become more involved? Too often, the good the local church does is not shared widely enough in order for everyone to enjoy what God is doing in the community. But more importantly, the church members cannot come into the powerful place of agreement if they are not aware of the issues and challenges facing them.

Every church service has a time for announcements. It may be more effective to provide congregations with a written status report every week or month. It could be available on a back table, mailed out on a monthly basis, or e-mailed to those who provide Web site addresses. It could also be available on the church's Web site. During the weekly service, the pastor could touch on the high points of the status report and encourage teammates to read the full report as well as contribute and participate. Pastors owe it to their congregational teammates to keep them informed, to trust them, and to allow them to help in the mission of the church.

If It Ain't in Writing, It Ain't ....

These clichés are used often in the business world:

- If it ain't in writing, it ain't as important as those things that are in writing.
- If it ain't in writing, it ain't ever going to happen.
- If it ain't in writing, it ain't as relevant as that which is.
- If it ain't in writing, it ain't serious enough to be worth our time.

Although the computer software industry espouses a paperless future, if we look around us, it is clear that everything truly important appears in writing, and many documents are often signed as well.

All public laws are in writing or they are not enforceable. Book club memberships and love letters to a sweetheart are so important that they are in writing. When we enter into an engagement for services with our clients, there is always some form of written contract or agreement in place beforehand. Even when we marry, there is legal paperwork.

All too often, after the project plan is written and approved and the contract is signed, the writing stops. This is a major reason for failures. Written understandings, directions, guidelines, instructions, status reports, and agreements—many people at different levels of responsibility refer to them. With the plentiful voicemail messages, the meetings and conferences, the lunchtime bargains, and the hallway compromises, none of which sees its way into print, there is no record for backup or confirmation of details, and the information is quickly forgotten or misunderstood.

Even when meeting minutes are taken, they are considered by most as a mere formality. But they are more than that. They are important project deliverables that should be circulated, discussed, and treated as governing documents. All too often, the secretary types up the minutes and files them away for some audit on a later date.

The purpose behind putting things in writing is to communicate the same ideas to all parties and ensure that they will be around for review, as needed. Situations change, people join and leave the team, and memories fade. In such cases, a written plan quickly gets new personnel informed and up to date.

Why is there such a widespread aversion to writing things down?

- The client says, "It really isn't necessary to do a lot of paperwork. I'd rather put my money to work on something more concrete."
- The project manager says, "Putting things in writing shows a lack of trust toward my client. It's like I'm insulting my client to insist on written documents."
- The boss says, "We had to cut our price in order to win this deal, so we cut out most of the administrative support. Just do the best you can without filling our files with paper."

Having things in writing protects relationships; it doesn't harm them. No project manager should ever give in to the idea of verbal agreements only. It is the quickest way to a problem with clients. If the client doesn't see the value of having things in writing and won't pay for it, we should do it without charge or cover the cost in other ways. No excuse is sufficient justification for not writing things down.

Creating a Crisis to Avoid a Larger Crisis

I have successfully insisted on taking written agreements one step further. I have stopped work on a project when the client was unwilling to document project events and decisions because I view this unwillingness as a symptom of something greater and more dangerous to the project. When a project is already in trouble and I don't take steps to correct the situation immediately, I'm not doing my job.

What sorts of things should be written down? Everything! Since this isn't practical, however, we can focus on these major documents, which cover the most important problem areas:

- All minutes of formal meetings
- All requests for assistance, guidance, or status and their responses
- All notifications of funding changes, schedule changes, personnel turnover, and potential problems
- All requests for additional resources of any kind (e.g., people, money, equipment)
- All disagreements with or alternate positions on project issues
- All issues or items needing action or tracking
- All changes to requirements or specifications or design documentation to ensure incorporation into the next revision of these documents
- All problems found during testing to ensure proper assignment, scheduling for rework, and resolution

Weekly Status Reports

I like weekly status reports. I like writing them, and I like receiving them. It is in the very nature of writing that we must think clearly, organize our thoughts into a logical flow, and then present the information in an understandable way. The status report is the one place where we managers can put down in writing our projects' most recent successes and accomplishments. It is where we can identify our plans and gain agreement from our clients that these plans are acceptable; it is where we can identify for resolution any problems we are encountering.

A simple status report format has three parts: progress, plans, and problems. With such a report in our hands, we can communicate effectively and efficiently with our clients, our bosses, and our project team members. We should also require a weekly status report from all our team leaders to keep us informed of significant advances and any new or nagging problems.

If our status reports are detailed enough, they will serve us well, not only as a record of the major agreements and changes in direction that came about over the previous week, but also as a reinforcement of our team's agreement on these issues.

As managers, we should write three different reports for our three different audiences: our client, our managers, and our project team. We should not delegate the writing of status reports to administrative staffers. They need to come directly from us, the managers. When we do so, we show our respect for our clients and our team members.

When writing each status report, we should remember our intended audience. A status report written for our managers might read differently and even contain some different information than a status report written for the project team or the client. We are not saying different things in each of these status reports. In each one, we are honestly giving the status of the project. Yet management usually wants to know more about dollars and deadlines than the project team does. The project team members want to know about the status of the problems they have raised or even the prospect of having to work on the following weekend.

Each written status report is accurate, honest, and open. It is also tailored to the needs and interests of its intended audience.

Status Reports from the Team

Our team members owe us an accounting, too. As project managers, we should make it a policy that all team leaders, including the assistant project manager, be required to provide a weekly status report.

If we can get them to agree, we should also request weekly reports from our supervisor and client to inform us of what is going on from their perspectives. Although these may be more difficult to obtain since we are the tail wagging the dog, we have nothing to lose by planting the seeds of how effective our weekly status reports are and how valuable theirs will be to us. After all, there can be no harvest without first sowing some seeds.

Finally, by sharing this information early enough with everyone involved, we can get their full support and agreement to achieve the goals. That, after all, is the ultimate reason for putting anything and everything of importance in writing. It helps all parties come to an agreement about the state of the project, the problems that must be solved, and the direction the project is going.

This agreement, via written status reports and other documents, is acquired on a weekly basis from all those involved. With this level and frequency of agreement, anything can be accomplished.

ATTITUDE ALIGNMENT:

Will Your Attitude Be to Write Everything Down?

1. **Have you ever had a disagreement with someone about a fact, a date, or a conversation?**
   - What the price of something was? When an anniversary or birthday is?
2. **Have you ever gone to an auto mechanic and NOT first received a written estimate for the repairs?**
   - Was the outcome, the final bill, what you expected, or were you surprised in some way?
   - Was the amount you owed less or more than you had been led to believe?
3. **Have you ever noticed even the little things you have to sign for every day?**
   - A FedEx or UPS delivery
   - A $30 purchase on a credit card
   - An order of Girl Scout cookies
4. **Describe a problem facing you today that would not have been a problem if things had been written down and agreed upon from the start.**

BE SLOW TO JUDGE

ATTITUDE 7

BE SLOW TO JUDGE

Do not judge so that you will not be judged. For in the way
you judge, you will be judged; and by your standard of measure,
it will be measured to you. Why do you look at the speck that
is in your brother's eye, but do not notice the log that is in your
own eye? Or how can you say to your brother, "Let me take the
speck out of your eye," and behold, the log is in your own eye?
You hypocrite, first take the log out of your own eye, and then
you will see clearly to take the speck out of your brother's eye.
Matt. 7:1–5 NASB

Perhaps the most difficult thing to do as leaders and
managers is to properly balance our reliance upon our own
skills, talents, experiences, and intuition when we must deal
with other people who are not measuring up. Before we
approach anyone with a perceived problem and a possible disciplinary action, we must take a step back and seek objectivity.

To one degree or another, we are all products of our experiences and surroundings. Our viewpoints on any issue are

tainted by them. We tend to view situations and other people from this personal perspective. For example, suppose we are morning people. We go to bed early and get up at dawn in order to begin checking off things on our to-do list. We forget that others are owls. They prefer to stay up late and sleep a little longer in the morning. Left unchecked, we could find it irritating when our teammates arrive an hour or two after we started working. We consider them lazy simply because they don't do things our way. We might conveniently "forget" that these people worked two hours after we left for home the night before.

Perception Is Not Reality

When I get involved in something, it is quite obvious from my body language, volume and speed of speech, and overall intensity that I am thrilled. Other people may not become as animated about their pleasure. That does not mean they are indolent, disinterested, or underachievers. Thankfully, all it means is that they are different.

Sarah was a unique member of one of my teams. She was quiet and introspective, whereas the rest of us were quite boisterous. She was a thorough planner, a rarity in the world of computer programmers. She preferred to lay everything out in a neat, orderly fashion and then plan for the building of her software. She was methodical and accurate. These positive traits were viewed by some of her teammates as faults. They found her too slow, too cautious, and too hesitant. They accused her of not pulling her own weight. They branded her a loner and not a team player because she rarely joined them for dinner or other social outings.

Sarah's former manager shared this assessment of her when she was assigned to work on my project. "She is a gifted programmer, but ... not a complete package."

I was tempted to take this manager's evaluation and treat Sarah accordingly. I felt I would have to keep after her to keep her on schedule. The fact that she was not as social as the others wouldn't bother me, but her job performance would. Thankfully, I remembered what it was like to be judged guilty before the trial and to be misunderstood. I remembered what it was like to be identified as a loner, which is certainly not a crime and which has nothing to do with being a team player.

I determined to wait and make my own judgment. I treated her like all the other team members. I negotiated her deliverables and her schedule. I gave her one of the more difficult programs to understand, design, write, and test. And ... I made her a team leader based upon her work seniority.

In the eyes of some, my giving Sarah so much responsibility was probably considered risky. Keeping to a strict schedule was extremely important, and providing quality deliverables by those dates was critical. How did it work out? Sarah was not the best team leader that year, and we struggled with that, but it was not due to a lack of effort or talent. Her work and leadership suffered because of low self-esteem acquired from the accumulated negative opinions about her. Because she didn't feel confident about her abilities, it was difficult for her to bring about respect from her team members. Her programming, however, was absolutely outstanding, and so was the quality of the assistance she gave her team members with their programming. Her methodical approach, although more time consuming up front, resulted in better and more efficient code in the end. Her code made it through testing more easily, and she beat all her deadlines. Because she was so efficient, she was able to pick up other activities in support of the project. In this case, her being a different kind of programmer was greatly to my and the team's advantage. She was, indeed, a complete package.

Over the course of the next year, Sarah and I worked closely on two more projects. Once her self-confidence was restored, she was a strong and enthusiastic leader. Today, she deals effectively with clients and team members. She still makes thorough plans before acting. She remains a bit of a loner and doesn't chum around after work on a regular basis. She has other interests, which help to define who she is.

Although it took more of my time to mentor her on the first project, it was well worth the effort. I followed the principles laid out in this book and treated her like I would want to be treated in her position. I provided encouragement, support, and respect. I waited to make my own assessment.

A Benevolent Judge

It takes practice to acquire the ability to make slow judgments. But as a project manager, I feel I have an added luxury of being able to work with a wide variety of talented people and help them grow into their full potential. In the past, I have turned down people for responsible positions because I knew their abilities and ambitions would require too much of my time to manage well. That may be one of my failings, but I prefer to train individuals for potential leadership positions who will take some of the burden from me rather than adding to it.

In other cases, I have purposely appointed rookies for leadership roles because of their potential for growth. Although initially it took more of my time, the rewards a few months down the road were worth the effort.

Dealing with the Judgments of Others

Once, I was faced with the challenge of contending with a project manager whose style was completely different from my own. He was accused, by some, of being dictatorial, condescending, erratic, and verbally abusive. These are not unusual management styles, but they are not to my liking. I cringed inwardly at the thought of friends having to work with him and tried my best to be in a position to protect them, if not day-to-day then at least where their career recommendations were concerned.

I worked with another manager who listened to gossip and false reports about various employees and treated them accordingly. As far as he was concerned, their erroneous reputation was set in concrete. He never revisited their work record. He simply wrote them off and placed the blame for his reactions on them. Once he had made a judgment, there was no way anyone could change his mind.

This insular behavior is dangerous because it sets up project managers for a fall from grace. It leads to hostility and a lack of trust between them and the members of their teams. That is exactly what happened to this manager. He reaped what he sowed. He was judged in the same harsh manner as he judged others, and his leadership suffered the consequences. The law of sowing and reaping came to pass: "For in the way you judge, you will be judged; and by your standard of measure, it will be measured to you" (Matt. 7:2 NASB).

Jesus was firm and expected high standards, but He was fair in His judgments. When He was presented with a woman who had been caught in adultery and was asked to punish her, He said, "He who is without sin among you, let him be the first to throw a stone at her" (John 8:7 NASB). Every one of us project managers will make mistakes at one time or another. When that happens, we will want understanding, advice, encouragement, and assistance from our supervisors. Therefore, we must determine to provide everyone with the same degree of respect. We must be benevolent and slow to find fault.

ATTITUDE ALIGNMENT:

Will Your Attitude Be to Be Slow to Judge?

1. **Have you ever gotten angry with another person?**
    - Your spouse? Your boss? Your best friend? Your child? A teammate? A neighbor? A fellow church member?
    - Was your judgment too swift?
2. **Did the swiftness of your judgment make it easier or more difficult to remedy?**
3. **Have you ever been misjudged or wrongly accused by another person?**
    - Your boss? Your spouse? Your parents? Your best friend? A neighbor? Your children?
4. **Have you ever wished for a way to remove a person's problems rather than wishing to write them off as a lost cause?**
5. **Has anyone ever written you off? Have you ever written anyone off before?**

ATTITUDE 8

BE FAIR IN DISCIPLINE

"Teacher, this woman has been caught in adultery, in the very act. Now in the Law Moses commanded us to stone such women; what then do you say?"... He straightened up and said to them, "He who is without sin among you, let him be the first to throw a stone at her."
John 8:4–5, 7 NASB
Brethren, even if anyone is caught in any trespass, you who are spiritual, restore such a one in a spirit of gentleness; each one looking to yourself, so that you too will not be tempted.
Gal. 6:1 NASB

When we think about discipline, we think about punishment. Children are spanked, given time-outs, or grounded. Many times, their favorite things are taken from them for a period of time. They are denied phone or television privileges, use of the family car, or overnights with friends. Adults are given traffic tickets for illegal parking or speeding, arrested for theft or disorderly conduct, divorced by unhappy spouses, and fired from their jobs for sundry reasons. Soldiers in the Army are given KP (kitchen patrol), extra guard duty, or endless pushups.

When we receive discipline from someone who holds the authority to deliver it, it is because we have broken rules we have agreed to uphold. Soldiers stand at attention and march in step, for a reason. They follow orders without question, for a reason. Employees at any level agree to follow project, department, or team guidelines and standards and abide by the established rules of the company, for a reason. Rules and guidelines are made for their protection and for the protection of the company. Many of the rules are safety rules, many are made to protect the company from theft of equipment, and many are made to assure that the quality of the company products remains as advertised.

To be self-disciplined is to choose to adhere to our own set of rules. We determine to walk away from an extra piece of chocolate cake. We determine to get up early every morning in order to exercise, meditate, read the Bible, work on our next book, feed our pets, or prepare breakfast for our children. We determine to be Christlike in our roles as leaders.

As leaders, we must dispense discipline when the members of our team don't follow company rules. We must determine the nature of the offense and prescribe the appropriate form and amount of reprimand. This is the worst part of our job, but the day is sure to come when we must take someone to task. How we go about the procedure is a key factor in our success as leaders and in the continued success of our workers as a team with a unified project goal.

If we have determined to present ourselves as leaders with Christlike qualities, how can we make a judgment and dole out a reprimand to a member of our team? If we follow the Golden Rule, do we even have the right to discipline? Can we be an effective Christian servant and respect our fellow worker ... and still chastise him or her? Of course we can. Discipline doesn't have to be backbreaking or ego-busting to be effective. It doesn't have to be dispensed in anger.

Company Guidelines

We have all been members of teams where we are instructed to follow published guidelines for our proper input on a project. These guidelines enumerate how to document our computer programs and how to write the code; they list the requirements for status reports, how to get problems resolved, the procedure for taking vacation and sick time, and many other things. Many company guidelines even include a dress code. When the rules aren't followed, disciplinary actions are taken.

Team members of every sport are instructed on the rules of the game, curfew requirements, uniform requirements, and practice schedules. When the rules aren't followed, disciplinary actions are taken. Towns and cities and counties and states and our country have rules and guidelines called laws. They are to be followed by every citizen. When they aren't, disciplinary measures are taken to get us back into agreement.

Company rules and guidelines are necessary in order to provide a safe and comfortable environment for everyone. They unify the playing field for every diverse player.

Discipline Is Essential to Success

Without written guidelines, we can anticipate problems with every team endeavor. There are as many opinions on every subject as there are noses. But no project can reach the finish line if everyone involved is allowed to do whatever he or she wishes, whenever and wherever. Written guidelines, read and signed by every participant, protect the rights of everyone. They allow every diverse and opinionated contributor to work beside other teammates in relative harmony and unity of purpose.

As leaders, we must use these guidelines properly ... as guiding principles and not as a means for excluding certain teammates. The rules and guidelines should be logical, achievable, and understandable by everyone.

Sooner or later, someone on the team will deviate from the rules, perhaps intentionally and perhaps not. We must deal with this deviation immediately and with the appropriate severity.

Our immediate reaction might be to blow up in anger. We might immediately think, "She did that on purpose!" or "He is intentionally undermining my authority!" Our challenge is to not overreact. If we must assume anything about the situation, then we should assume that we do not have all the facts. After all, we are determined to be a leader who is slow to judge.

None of us is perfect, and we all make honest mistakes. If a team member has made a mistake, we must first collect the facts and then re-examine the policies that were violated.

Hopefully, they are in writing and are clear and understandable. Hopefully, the offending team member has signed a document saying he or she has read and understood the rules.

Next, we must determine if the supposed offense actually fits within the guidelines or if it could be interpreted differently, depending on the other person's point of view. Was the offender made aware of the guidelines at the start of the project? Is every other worker on the project following the policies in the way they were intended? By taking the time to answer these questions, we turn our attention away from the individual and focus our energy on the problem.

We must determine if the fault lies with the procedures and the process or with the individual's interpretation of them.

We gain more than an answer to these questions by pursuing this course of action. Rather than lashing out with immediate and shoot-from-the-hip judgment and disciplinary action, we maintain the respect of the entire team. Of course, if the wrongdoing put anyone's life at risk or caused serious damage to the project's success, the offender may need to be removed from the project while a more comprehensive investigation is made. A good manager can never place his personal standards or demeanor above the safety of his crew or project.

Most of us are not accustomed to being given the benefit of the doubt. Many times, we are falsely accused based upon circumstantial evidence. We all remember managers who were more interested in removing the symptom than solving the underlying problem. As a Christlike leader, we must be better than that for the sake of our team members and our project.

And what if we break a rule or guideline? What should we do? Ask for forgiveness. Why would we ask our teammates to forgive us? Because we were wrong! And our being wrong will undoubtedly cause the team to have to work harder and longer. No one looks over our shoulder to see if we are conforming to our standards. We managers pretty much chart our own course. When we make mistakes, it is important to show our team members that we understand how honest mistakes can happen. We need to show them that we are fair and honest and worthy of their respect and admiration.

Most of the problems that occur among team members and on work projects have to do with misunderstandings, mistakes, and accidents. Very few are due to maliciousness.

The Troublesome 20%

What about those individuals who know the routine and simply refuse to follow it—the troublesome 20% who cause 80% of the problems? Very often, their behavior is a symptom of something much larger and more important than the success of the project. It may be tied to how they feel about themselves and their personal goals. Many times, they are wrestling with conflicting goals and conflicts between their personal and work lives.

Getting to Know Ray

I served in the Army in West Germany with Ray, who was forever violating the rules. Even the simplest duties, which were not all that complicated, seemed to befuddle him. It wasn't a matter of intelligence because he was extremely well educated.

I was Ray's team leader, and his behavior caused me more than a little concern and grief—concern that I was having difficulty understanding his untoward behavior, and grief because my superiors were holding me accountable for him.

For a while, I tried to cover for him by doing his work for him. Then, I tried the normal Army sergeant routine of yelling and badgering. Neither method worked. I didn't want to see Ray fail, but he needed to be more effectively disciplined and better motivated.

That was the key ... his lack of motivation. Ray was not conforming to the rules because he wasn't motivated to do so. I spent time getting to know Ray.

As I got to know Ray, it became clear to me that he was not a happy person. He was disillusioned and discouraged, and he felt trapped by his own devices. He had joined the Army with erroneous expectations. He was surprised to learn that his intellect was not as evident to everyone else and that he had not received the level of respect he had anticipated. He thought someone with his advanced training and mathematical and linguistic abilities should have been given a more suitable position.

Unfortunately, the unit to which we were assigned had no need for his special talents. It needed soldiers who could perform mechanical maintenance on Jeeps, trucks, and tracking vehicles as well as survive on a battlefield. The duties were diverse, but few of them were what anyone would consider topics of interest to a genius like Ray.

Our discussions were fruitful, however. I learned that Ray felt betrayed by the Army and completely out of place as a soldier. He felt trapped and powerless to do anything about it.

I shared my own experiences with Ray, my own sense of futility in many situations and how I had worked through them. I opened up and let him know there were others who felt the same way, although our reasons may not be the same as his. I assured him we had each eventually come to closure. We were able to function without selling our souls.

Ray saw an avenue of escape. He discovered he could perform and even excel at his mundane Army duties while keeping his identity as a scholar. The two ideas were not incompatible. He participated in field training exercises with enthusiasm and became a model soldier. He did everything anyone asked of him with efficiency and alacrity. Whenever he had some free time between shifts and move-outs, he occupied himself by reading from his latest textbook on some lofty subject, totally oblivious to his surroundings. He found he could perform the lesser challenging activities of his Army profession without sacrificing intellectual stimulation.

Later in his tour, Ray became an effective team leader himself. He always took care of the men and women assigned to him, and his missions were accomplished with high morale.

Golden Rule, Again

The lesson to be learned from this example is that we are all basically alike. We have doubts and fears and desires and opinions and goals. They simply vary from person to person. While we may fully understand the importance of teamwork and following rules, we sometimes lose our enthusiasm and attention to detail. We're troubled about how we got to where we are. We're depressed about it. We can't see a way out.

A leader/manager with Christlike attitudes will look for these underlying reasons for inappropriate behavior and make an earnest attempt to change the attitude of the individual needing discipline.

Everyone we work with is highly motivated and as enthusiastic about the same project-related things as we are. If we believe this about our teammates and never doubt their willingness or capability to contribute, we will receive the same in kind. If we show them trust, respect, support, and compassion, we will receive the same in kind.

No Public Inquisitions

Scripture tells us that if someone is breaking the rules and causing problems, we should go to that person in private to discuss the matter. This is sound advice.

Effective approaches we might use include taking the troubled individual to lunch, talking behind a closed office door, or taking a walk outside. The meeting should be comfortable and friendly. There are very few things the person could have done to completely damage the project, and personal animosities among teammates can be repaired. There is no need for an insensitive and accusatory inquisition. If we are being an efficient manager, we will discover this anomalous behavior in plenty of time to correct it. If we're not, the full responsibility for the problem is ours, not the team member's.

We should immediately set the tone of the discussion by laying out our perceptions of the person's behavior, being careful not to use judgmental words. We should use words and phrases such as "I would have thought ...," "How did you interpret what I said ...," or "How can I make this less ambiguous ...?" Our goal should be to create an open dialogue, encouraging truthfulness and trust. Our main concern is how the guidelines could have been misinterpreted by the individual. We should ask for a detailed response and listen closely to the answers. If handled in this manner, the person will eventually open up and share the real problem ... the one that caused the infraction.

No Private Executions

In the rare instance where an individual is intentionally violating the rules for no good reason, we must act decisively. Everything we do or don't do sends a message ... plants a seed. If we let this problematic behavior go unpunished, the message to the rest of the team and the client is that our rules don't matter.

Once we decide to discipline a team member, we must make the consequence public. A secret, hidden disciplinary action is the same as no punishment at all in the eyes of those watching. We need to establish that the rules of the project are important and there are consequences for violating them.

This doesn't mean that we publicly punish the individual. We should never verbally reprimand anyone during a project or staff meeting or place such an action into a status report. However, we must make it clear to everyone involved that the violation was noticed, the person was held accountable, and the situation has been corrected. The point is to ensure that everyone knows adherence to the rules is required. There are no exceptions. There are consequences for violating them. Within these guidelines, we leaders must be as caring and respectful as we can. We want the individual to reform the offending behavior. We are not dispensing revenge, but rather discipline. There is a great difference between correction and revenge.

Assuming the offense is grave enough, we might consider removing the person from the project. That is usually sufficiently severe punishment, and it certainly sends all the right messages to the rest of the team.

ATTITUDE ALIGNMENT:

Will Your Attitude Be to Be Fair in Discipline?

1. **Are you responsible for or held accountable for the behavior of others?**
   - Does your boss expect you to ensure the job performance of those assigned to you? Do you have children at home?
   - Do you have influence on how others might be treated?

2. **Are you ever asked to provide input into another person's performance review?**
   - Can you help or harm another person's career or personal advancement?
   - Do you have the capability to enhance or hinder a person's career or personal goals by the tasks and responsibilities you give that person? Or withhold from that person?

3. **A leader has tremendous responsibilities. Some are expected as part of the job, but others, such as disciplining team members, are not. How will you change as you adopt this leadership attitude? What changes will your team members see in you?**

ATTITUDE 9

MAINTAIN PERSPECTIVE

*For what will it profit a man if he gains the whole world
and forfeits his soul?
Or what will a man give in exchange for his soul?*
Matt. 16:26 NASB

I love to work with eager, talented men and women who are what we call zealots. They are a joy to work with. We can never ask too much of them, and they always give us more than we ask for. They are committed to the team, the project, and everyone's success. They are willing to admit mistakes and learn from them. They are intense, driven, and high-strung. They are also a challenge to direct and instruct, but what champion isn't? Nevertheless, as managers, we need to be aware of at least two dangers.

Tempering the Zealots

We may be tempted to work these eager beavers so hard that we burn them up. Since they seem so happy to work late every night and on weekends and holidays, we take advantage of their attitudes "for the good of the project." Since they are willing to do double shifts, we don't hesitate to change directions midstream into the project. Eventually, they hit the wall and have no more to give, even though they are willing to try. Our project may come to a swift halt if we need to look for new people to take over.

Second, we may be tempted to take over the lives of our zealots. They find so much stimulation and satisfaction from working on exciting, well-run projects that too often they are willing to forget about other important things ... friends, family, and relaxation. We must accept part of the blame for their failed family lives and lack of outside interests if we take advantage of their passion for work. As Christlike leaders, we mustn't give in to the temptation to take over our zealots by encouraging unhealthy obsessions for the good of the team.

Managers prefer to work with those who are devoted, enthusiastic, and talented, especially when the alternative is to work with those who simply put in their time to collect a steady paycheck. If we want to win the race, we like to work with team members who don't need the whip. But it is part of our job to maintain a proper perspective. Happy and content team members produce more in fewer hours.

Producing Contented and Productive Team Members

If we leaders are doing our jobs properly, our teammates will enjoy working on the project, will give their all during well-defined work hours and a few occasions of overtime, and will feel free to live equally satisfying lives outside the work-place. We will provide daily feedback on their performances and give them increasing responsibilities. They will know they are contributing something worthwhile to their teammates, to themselves, and to their families. But ... they will also feel free to play as hard as they work with their friends and family members.

Too often, project team members feel like mushrooms, always kept in the dark and never part of the mainstream of the project. Or they feel like machines turning out plans, designs, and products with automaton efficiency. They fear that if they aren't spending every possible minute at their desks trying to see daylight and cranking out more than their colleagues, they will be seen as slackers, and their careers will suffer. When we treat them like the human beings they are, show our appreciation for their excellent work, and then encourage them to spend the weekend with their families, they are going to return to the workplace with renewed vigor, eager to prove their worth to the project and to the company. Happy teammates are productive teammates.

Man Overboard!

Some members of our project team will show their appreciation by going overboard. Having a taste of what it means to be valued and experiencing the pleasure of producing an important part of a usable project, they talk about wanting to get a company-provided computer in order to work at home on weekends. They might bring in a cot in order to sleep at the office. They might eat at their desk rather than take a lunch break off the premises or in the employee lunchroom.

We managers who espouse Christlike qualities will take an interest in such team members. We will engage them in conversation to determine if they are doing anything after hours such as reading books that don't relate to the project, working out at the gym, or pursuing their interests in painting, writing, sculpting, sailing, biking, or running. Caring and supportive managers, like us, want our teammates to spend quality time with their loved ones.

Showing an interest in the personal lives of our team members demonstrates that we possess a proper perspective and want them to do likewise. As leaders, we demonstrate to those in our charge how to juggle their work lives with their personal lives. This is especially important if our team members are young and new in their careers. They are extremely concerned about doing a good job, impressing us, and proving themselves to their peers with whom they are often extremely competitive. It is not enough to be the world's best programmer analyst or teacher or chef or nurse or Salvation Army volunteer. A wider perspective will prepare us for the inevitable ... the end of the project.

Balance Schmalance!

I am not advocating a strict balance between work and play—eight hours of sleep, eight hours of work, and eight hours of quality time with the family every day of every year. Trying to achieve a balance actually detracts from our work performance. Seldom do people say, "You know, I'm playing too hard and need to put more into my work." Usually they say, "I'm working too hard and need to make more time for play." Both are good for us, but if we work too hard at striking a balance, we are apt to put less effort into both.

If we are the manager of a large project with numerous deliverables required every few months, and if our teammates, wishing to have more balance in their lives, begin to play harder, we may run into trouble. Perhaps one individual takes karate classes on Tuesday and Thursday nights and another enrolls in a Saturday MBA program. Someone else volunteers to coach his son's softball team on Monday nights, and another individual takes a course in English as a second language on Wednesday nights. While these are beneficial and worthwhile and we would normally encourage our teammates to pursue them, they cannot be considered a balance. They will jeopardize our project. Why? Because not everything is equally important. Sometimes there are priorities, and they must take more of our time. That means something else has to give way, at least over the short term.

Goal Setting with a Twist

How can we encourage our teammates to pursue these other interests and still require them to put their job first? We take time with each of our team members to discuss their objectives for the upcoming year or for the duration of the project, whichever is shorter. This is management by objectives, but with an important twist.

We ask each teammate to make two lists of at least five items per list, one for their professional goals and the other for their personal goals. Then we ask them to prioritize the goals on each list, from the most important to the least. Now we ask them to merge the two prioritized lists to make one. The result of this exercise is important and useful information for us to know if we are to be proficient in our roles as project managers. If an individual's first professional priority is to maximize the bonus plan, and his first personal priority is to spend more time with his family, a difficult and conflicting problem exists. The individual must answer the question, "Is it worth sacrificing time with my family over the short term to earn the maximum amount of money, which may improve the quality of our lives?" The answer to this question places the two items in proper relationship to each other.

Our next role is to discuss each team member's list in a private conference. In fact, review of the list should occur once a quarter. Priorities change with changing perspectives. These conferences empower managers because the more we know about our teammates, the more resourceful we will be when using their talents, drive, and interests for the benefit of the project and the company. Also, we'll work toward satisfying at least some of each teammate's goals. In this way, we can combat the two dangers of burn up and burn out. Our expression of interest in their non-work activities encourages them to have a life outside the company.

Remember, Jesus Christ came to save the whole person—body, soul, and spirit. As we work toward becoming Christlike leaders, we would do well to follow His example. He enjoyed life so much that He once was accused of enjoying it too much. He took time away from his ministerial work to socialize with friends, to attend weddings and dinners, and to go alone into the desert and mountains to pray. Mostly, He went out of His way to help people. He healed their bodies. He raised their spirits. He gave them individual attention. He had the proper perspective on life. Not arbitrary balance ... but order.

ATTITUDE ALIGNMENT:

Will Your Attitude Be to Maintain Perspective?

1. **Are you a berserker, a workaholic?**
   - Do you get excited about your job to the point of being late for dinner at home? Would you rather eat while you work? Does it ever bother you to work on weekends?

2. **Do you have a berserker on the team?**
   - Do you find yourself encouraging him or her to work harder and longer than others on the team? Do you give berserkers preferential treatment?

3. **Do you wish you knew more about each team member?**
   - What are their hobbies and interests? How did each one spend last weekend? Which ones are in graduate school?

4. **Adopting this attitude may be difficult if you are the berserker type. That's okay. Commit to the attitude first and then foster it in your team. Where will you start? What needs to change first in your daily and weekly routine?**

ATTITUDE 10

Observe a Sabbath Rest

By the seventh day God completed His work which He had
done, and He rested on the seventh day from all
His work which He had done.
Gen. 2:2–3 NASB
Jesus said to them, "The Sabbath was made for man, and
not man for the Sabbath."
Mark 2:27 NASB

A definition of mentally deranged is trying to do the same thing over and over again while expecting a different result. If we stare at a piece of buggy code for hours and hours at a time and still can't see the problem, we need a different strategy. If we lock our team in a room until we can find an answer to a problem or come to agreement on an issue, we are probably wasting time. If we work nonstop—twelve hours a day, seven days a week—for months, we may well lose interest in the job altogether. Such a thoughtless policy is dangerous to the team and to the project.

Human beings are not designed to work incessantly. It is unnatural for us to do so. We need to refresh our minds. We need sleep in order to have enough energy to work during the day. We need joy and laughter in order to prevent depression and gloom. On too many projects, we managers insist on long workdays, weekend duty, and all-nighters. These tactics only work when they are employed sparingly and by design. A project culture of such a work ethic renders team members totally ineffective.

Rest—A Critical Success Factor

"Remember the Sabbath day, to keep it holy" (Deut. 5:12 HCSB). The quoted biblical text suggests that something within us requires a Sabbath ... a day of rest. We shouldn't think of these periods of rest as something to be observed because the labor union forced management to provide them or because a forty-hour work week is the norm in the United States. We should think of them as a necessity for the maintenance of health and vitality, productivity and efficiency.

Animals, Soldiers, and Programmers

All plants and animals need rest. It seems like a peculiar requirement. The sun doesn't rest in its production of light and heat. The oceans don't rest in their waning and ebbing. The planets continue revolving in their orbits. But animals and birds sleep, as do reptiles and even ants. Evergreen plants go dormant for a period of time in order to maintain their health and efficiency.

The natural prey of African lions knows when it is safe to be around them and when it is not. Lions don't hunt incessantly but only when they are hungry. Imagine the lion's stress—not to mention that of their prey—if it had to hunt all the time, nonstop.

Ages ago, military commanders realized a strong force could not be maintained if their soldiers had to fight continually without periods of rest. The trench warfare of World War I was a terrible thing. Many more soldiers died of disease and neglect than by enemy bullets or bayonets. In most modern wars, battles are orchestrated affairs that are well thought out, choreographed, and timed. Troops on both sides are rested and given time to prepare, physically and mentally. The actual fighting is concluded in a matter of minutes or hours. On rare occasions, a battle might rage for days, but then a rest cycle is imposed. The troops rest in order to survive. Whole units are taken off the battle line for the purpose of restoring strength of body and mind. In the workplace, somehow our lessons from Scripture, the animal kingdom, and warfare have been lost.

Twenty-one Days without a Shower

When I was a consultant for Oracle Corporation, the company sent me to England to work on a project. It was my first time there, and I looked forward to the weekends to see some of London and the English countryside. Unfortunately, it was not to happen. A design review was scheduled, allowing us only three weeks to prepare. Our entire team worked a total of 270 hours in a twenty-one-day period, excluding commuting time to and from the client's site. I did not see anything of England,

and I am certain I did not do my very best work. I was too long in the battle.

During the late 1970s, I served in an Army infantry support unit in West Germany. My unit was required to participate each year in numerous field exercises (simulated combat situations). During these exercises, we went without sleep for upwards of seventy-two hours. I distinctly remember going without a shower for twenty-one days during one of these war games. We slept on the ground in a tent or under our rain poncho, or we slept sitting up in our vehicles, awaiting orders to move out to our new location. We went without a hot meal for a week at a time. Our commanders understood, however, that every few days, they needed to give us a breather to catch up on sleep and food and to bathe in our helmets. Even on a training mission, a break was important.

How does this example relate to software applications project development? How does it relate to the management of a softball team or the management of a church project?

Taking a Break ... Fixes Things

Very few of us have the ability to completely "forget" our work project responsibilities. They remain in our subconscious and intrude on our other thoughts, no matter how hard we try to dismiss them.

Although I work at least ten hours a day at my office, I live this project around the clock. I think about the project as I drive to and from work, talk about the project with my wife in the evening, and dream about it in my sleep. To do this for weeks and months on end is destructive. Without a respite, my stress will build to dangerous levels, allowing battle fatigue to set in.

Even knowing that the project is "work and not war" is not enough. For project managers, a project often feels more like war. We have deadlines to meet and a never-ending stream of problems, personnel issues, and contracting issues to contend with. It is difficult to get away from them ... to put them out of our minds.

Thankfully, there is the law of sowing and reaping. If we want to reap time away from the project, we must plant something that will produce the harvest of time. We do this by planting time in the lives of our team members. We are continually asked by them if they can get away from the project for a few days ... for training purposes. And based upon the needs of the immediate schedule and our attitude of maintaining our perspective regarding work and play, we generally encourage the teammate to take the time off. If another teammate wants a long weekend, we look at his individual schedule and our schedule as a whole, solicit a commitment so the individual will not get behind, and then approve the time off.

We remain attentive to how our teammates are doing physically and mentally and how well they are performing their jobs. It is not uncommon for us to tell those who appear burned up and burned out to go home. We forbid them to think about the project for a couple of days.

Not only does this help team morale, but we reap a benefit as well. After these brief Sabbath breaks, the individuals return refreshed, re-energized, more creative, and more productive. We need to do the same for ourselves.

Necessary Diversions

Another way for us to deal with our stress is to do something that is sufficiently divorced from the project. Do something that will help us forget the project for at least a few minutes. This can be something as simple as taking a walk, shooting a few minutes of basketball, or enjoying an ice cream cone.

I like to spend time with my animals. My family currently has two horses, two dogs, and two cats. Feeding and caring for them is relaxing and rejuvenating. Their lives are simple and routine. They rely on us for everything. They are easily pleased and, for the most part, readily demonstrate their appreciation for what we do for them. Pets provide immediate gratification for our efforts, something we don't often see from people. In any case, playing with my dogs is a great way to temporarily forget about my next project deadline.

Beware the Guilty Sabbath!

Several years ago, my family and I attended a church where the pastor emphasized service to others. I felt I could contribute in several areas. However, it wasn't long before these activities meant being at the church six nights a week and twice on Sundays. My family life suffered because I had to rush off immediately after dinner for some extracurricular activity or meeting. My personal interests were put on indefinite hold. Finally, my energy, enthusiasm, and ability to serve were hampered by fatigue. No activity received the best I had to offer because I had spread myself too thin. I was unproductive. I needed a reprieve from responsibilities and deadlines. I needed time for myself.

Of course, when I told the pastor I would be unable to help out as much as I had in the past, the "guilt" set in. No one can make us feel guilty. We do that to ourselves. We needn't feel guilty about taking time for ourselves. It is difficult to keep the proper perspective when we are both a leader and a servant, but it is absolutely vital to take time for ourselves, for our own sake and for the benefit of the team.

Manage the Project or Be Managed By It

There is another temptation facing us as managers: the temptation to believe that we are indispensable and that unless we do it or watch it being done, it will not get done. The truth is that everyone can be replaced, even us.

If our project is in such a state that we can't be gone for a day or two or a team member can't attend a week of training (given sufficient notice) without it falling apart, then shame on us! We are already failing as managers. Things are seriously wrong, and we are ignoring the facts. The very fact that we can't get away means that the project is in serious trouble. Too much is yet to be answered or determined. Too many things are changing on a daily basis. Too few people on the project have been entrusted with the authority to make decisions. These are the signs of a serious problem. Do not think that so long as we are there every day, these problems don't exist.

We should plan our projects to enable proper treatment of the needs of our very human team members. And that includes our needs as well. Even workhorses and racehorses get a day off! We need to plan these times of rest and regeneration into our projects. If we don't, then we aren't serving our teams well. We aren't serving our clients as we should. We aren't serving our boss as we should. And ... we aren't taking care of ourselves as we should.

God worked six days and took the seventh day off for rest and enjoyment of the fruits of His labor.

ATTITUDE ALIGNMENT:

Will Your Attitude Be to Observe a Sabbath Rest?

1. **Do you often plan working lunches for the team?**
   - Do you do this because the project schedule cannot afford to have people taking time off for lunch? Do you intend to continue this practice for more than a few weeks?

2. **Did you fail to take your vacation this year?**
   - Do you think that you are too important to the project to be away for a few days? How about for a couple of weeks?

3. **Has anyone canceled training or vacation "for the good of the project"?**
   - Was the training canceled even though it was a project-related topic? Was the vacation canceled even though it had been properly scheduled in advance?

4. **Observing a Sabbath rest is not the same as taking a sabbatical. The rule of the Sabbath is that it is one day out of every seven. You cannot carry them over into the next month or year or decade. What is it going to look like as you adopt this attitude? What must change first?**

ATTITUDE 11

Have a Vision

Where there is no vision, the people are unrestrained.
Prov. 29:18 NASB
Write the Vision; make it plain on tablets,
so he may run who reads it.
Hab. 2:2 ESV

This attitude—having a vision—is one of the more mysterious ones. Why it works, we don't know. It just works.

Everyone needs to strive for the achievement of a goal. Goals make life worth living. They encourage us to improve our talents and stretch and challenge our intellectual and physical abilities. Successes, triumphs, and accomplishments of all kinds—big or small, significant or not so significant—are satisfying. Although they take careful planning and constant effort, they make life worthwhile. That is why it is so important to have a vision for our project team. No, it is more than that. It is imperative that we have a compelling vision.

Almost every activity is a project. A team project is a group effort to achieve a specific result in a given amount of time. We must know what we want to have happen and when. Then, we must pull together the resources to make it happen.

This, then, is the vision for our project. But in order to be a vision, it must have a requisite level of clarity and detail. We must know what it will look and feel like when the vision is realized. We must know the details. We must be able to describe the vision in tangible terms so every member of the team can relate to it.

A vision that cannot be articulated to this level of detail is no vision at all and can never be a persuasive vision. If we cannot excite every member about the importance and relevancy of the project, the project team will flounder; its members will be distracted, disorganized, and ... unrestrained.

Have a Compelling Vision

Our vision for the project can and must be compelling. It is not enough to say that the project's purpose—vision—is to build a client relationship management system. Why build it? Why build it now? Why build it the way we intend to build it? Why not build it some other way? Who will benefit when it is built? In what ways will they benefit?

A Vision Tells Us Why

Why create a church building committee? What is the rationale for the committee? Why does the church need to add on to the existing building? What will the extra floor space be used for? Who will benefit? What will the church be able to do that it cannot do now?

Why form a new Boy Scout or Girl Scout troop? Why start a new company or business? Why form another soccer ream, softball team, or football team? Why study American history in the eighth grade? Why have a formal wedding? Why start a Bible study or prayer group? Why take a family vacation to Rome?

When asked why he climbed the mountain, the old mountain climber replied, "Because it was there." This is not enough of a reason to do anything. It isn't exciting or compelling enough to encourage us to go through the pain and effort required to reach the top.

The same is true of our projects. Our teammates are looking for a legitimate cause to be a part of. It is our job as their leader to give them that compelling reason. Without a convincing reason and a clearly described project vision, we are unlikely to formulate a team of enthusiastic workers. They will not be as motivated as they could be, should be, or need to be. It is the manager's job, the coach's job, and the teacher's job to provide every team member with a deep sense of mission and the clear vision of how their efforts will cause good things to happen.

Moving from Vision to Plan

Once our vision is established, the next step is to lay out the path for getting from where we are to the realization of our vision. There is a useful tool for creating this path or plan. It is a Work Breakdown Structure (WBS). A WBS is the splitting up of the vision into a hierarchy of activities. When these are complete, the vision will have been achieved.

For example, if I wish to plan out what happens every morning for a family of four, it might look something like this.

Task 1. Get out of bed
Task 2. Shave
Task 3. Take a shower
Task 4. Comb hair
Task 5. Brush teeth
Task 6. Get dressed
Task 7. Start car
Task 8. Drive kids to school
Task 9. Drive to work
Task 10. Feed the cat

But this plan is not enough. It does not assign tasks to anyone in particular. Dad certainly shaves, but little six-year-old Susie doesn't. Who drives the kids to school? Who drives to work? Who feeds the cat? Cat? What cat?

The WBS is not meant to give us these details. Much more work is required to enable a team to turn a vision into reality.

Managing to the Vision

The process of moving from vision to achievement of the vision is a process of project management. We take a vision, break it down into its simplest pieces, assign these pieces to real people, figure out which piece must come before another piece or which pieces can happen at the same time, and then come to an agreement with each team member on how long it will take them to get their piece of the vision completed.

This process provides us with the strongest project management tool available—a detailed plan and schedule. A vision not supported by a credible schedule is doomed. A vision with a credible schedule is a powerful force that will forge an effective team whose only purpose is the attainment of its shared vision. Powerful stuff!

Exceptional managers have a certain attitude. They know the value of a vision for the team and realize that in order to achieve the vision, they must provide an agreeable and detailed schedule that every member will follow.

A Vision Must Be Visible

During a football game, is the team aware of the clock? Do the players know how much time is left in each quarter? The half? The game? Do they know where they stand in terms of winning or losing the game? Do they know the score?

Of course they do. They know all these things. Most of the information is prominently displayed in bright numbers on a huge scoreboard at the end of the stadium. Our projects are very much like games. We need to know the schedule and the score.

I gave the example of a project that had been grossly under-bid in terms of how much programming we had to deliver in a six-month timeframe. What I didn't mention is that another company had been working on the project before I arrived on the scene. This previous company had performed excellent work, had been extremely attentive to the needs of the users, had taken great pains to document everything, and so forth. But the project had been going on for almost three years with no end in sight—three years with nothing tangible to show for it.

An audit of the situation showed there was no firm schedule for the accomplishment of anything. In fact, any due dates were only target dates, not deadlines. There was no pain or penalty for missing them.

This situation was viewed as good customer service. Allowing the client to continually add and change things was a good thing. The team never met a scheduled date, but the client was happy and getting what they wanted, or so they thought. They eventually became unhappy when no concrete results were forthcoming and from the expenditure of so much time, effort, and money.

The best customer service is to lead customers toward the completion of their stated goals. These goals must be considered sacred; they must be defended, consistent, and unswerving. Changing a stated goal midstream in a pro-ject should require approval from the very highest levels of authority; otherwise, the project is doomed to shifting goals, which cause serious schedule and cost overruns and eventual failure.

A Vision Needs a Deadline

Without a specific deadline, very little gets done.

Remember the speech President John F. Kennedy gave about the United States putting men on the Moon? In it, he set a time limit. He wanted us to get to the Moon before the end of decade—the 1960s.

What a master stroke! Not only did he help the country understand the value of such an achievement, but he also defined a time limit for its accomplishment. This placed it in perspective, provided a much needed sense of urgency, assigned the mission a high priority, and automatically provided a means against which to measure progress and ultimate success. The same is necessary for software development, construction, church, sports, and family projects.

Once, I was called in to analyze and design a complex integration logistics database for the U.S. Air Force Missile Command. The Air Force had contracted with a small company to build a first-of-its-kind system. The original schedule was extremely ambitious and poorly communicated to the contractor. There was no agreement by any of the parties involved. In fact, there was agreement only on the fact that everyone disagreed with the schedule.

In defense of the contractor's project team, there were extenuating circumstances and a lot of denial going on. Yet no matter what the extenuating circumstances, beginning work on a project without formulating and requiring adherence to a schedule is a recipe for failure.

A schedule is a best estimate, given limited information. But if it is a best estimate, then there should be some pain associated with missing it. It is preferable to have a scheduled deadline and miss it than to not have a schedule at all. It is understandable that unforeseen circumstances may mandate the slipping of a schedule for some period of time, but a new schedule must be established immediately ... and followed.

Not all schedules fail. There is power in setting a goal and working hard to achieve it. Something comes into the situation to help the process. It includes a sense of urgency and a sacrificial attitude on the part of the team members to meet their commitments. Remember, if all concerned have done their work right, the schedule dates are agreed upon and enforced.

Can you imagine a coach going to his team and asking them to give 110% to the game and not have it understood that the game was only sixty minutes long? What if the game were to be played under some arbitrary, secret completion time? Can anyone give 110% indefinitely? Of course not. It is better to say, "Give me your best efforts for the next sixty minutes. That's all I ask. If you do that, then no one can beat us."

People Can Do Amazing Things for a Worthy Cause over the Short Term

I am a Vietnam-era veteran, and I remember the way the war was conducted. I did not serve in Vietnam, but I talked to many who did. The typical day was spent doing noncombat-related duties such as training, KP, latrine duty, guard duty, sleeping, or whatever. The actual number of hours spent in the midst of battle was very small for the vast majority of the fighting men and women serving there.

It had to be this way. The times of actual combat were intense; enormous fire power was being used, vast amounts of destruction was occurring, and to continue for the entire year-long tour would have been impossible for anyone. Tremendous deeds of heroism were performed, but it seemed there was always an immediate goal for which they were fighting and suffering. If they could only hold out through the night, if they could capture this hill or that village, if they could merely make it back to the helicopter pickup point ... everything would be all right. Every soldier knew exactly how many days he had left until his discharge. He had a master plan and a scheduled end date, and they gave him hope— hope that he could make it, one day at a time. He had a vision; he knew what his assigned tasks were ... and he had a schedule.

Parents know that a baby will be born nine months after conception. Parents have a goal and a deadline. The baby will arrive on a particular day. The mother-to-be schedules regular examinations by her doctor. The doctor schedules regular blood tests and ultrasound procedures. Everyone knows exactly what will happen when and in what sequence. Nothing is left to chance.

During this nine-month period, relatives and friends are informed of the impending birth, baby showers are scheduled and given, shopping trips are taken to purchase furniture, clothes, bottles, pacifiers, and all the rest. It is not enough to simply sit back and wait for the blessed event. There is a goal and a vision and a schedule.

We are all capable of tremendous accomplishments, given the proper set of circumstances. But offer us no hope of success, no small incremental milestones that we can accomplish, and we become discouraged and disheartened. It is our job as leaders to make sure that we motivate. We can do this if we take our plan and schedule to them and do whatever is necessary to ensure that each of them understands the goal and agrees to work toward its achievement.

The Schedule as Stress Reliever

A good schedule relieves stress. Perhaps it isn't a stress reliever for the project manager, but it is for the team. It is a known fact that one of the greatest causes of stress is uncertainty. What can cause more uncertainty on a project than to not know for sure what you are expected to accomplish in what timeframe or with what resources?

A schedule is a magic tool that will motivate, invigorate, and comfort our teammates. At first, no one wants to sign on for a deadline. A deadline implies pressure and anxiety. But another word for this type of pressure is guidance. Most of us work better when provided with proper guidance. Having a schedule with deadlines is a means of gently gaining the very best out of ourselves and others.

The Manager's Scorecard

The project schedule is the project manager's personal score-card. It shows us at our best or worst. The schedule tells all. As a leader, we are like a mechanic who works at fine-tuning each of our team members to encourage peak performance. Many of us would rather sit behind our desks and be served. The truly exceptional among us are always listening to our engines, catering to them, caring for them, and tuning and tweaking them for better performance. Only in this way can our vision for the project be achieved.

Jesus Christ gave us the world's most compelling vision. He offered to us the opportunity to be in harmony with God the Father. He laid out the ultimate objective, the highest achievement, the grand finale. He told us how we could be in constant, intimate communion with God Almighty, forever. He told us what the plan was, how we could participate in the plan, and what the final outcome would be if we joined His team. It was such a compelling vision that it changed the course of human history and reshaped human civilization and government. His vision served to lift every human being out of the despair and uncertainty of a world without God and to a place of love, hope, and dignity.

A compelling vision is a powerful thing, indeed.

ATTITUDE ALIGNMENT:

Will Your Attitude Be to Have a Vision?

1. **Are you the leader of a group of people, a team?**
   - Are you a manager, pastor, coach, supervisor, leader, foreman, chairperson, president, business owner, military commander, study leader, or parent?
2. **Does the team you lead have a purpose?**
   - Is the team supposed to accomplish something specific? Is there a schedule to keep or a deadline to meet?
3. **Does the team look to you for their overall direction and purpose?**
   - Do you feel responsible for the team? Is it your job to set the team's strategy, goals, and methods?
4. **It is very likely that those above you in leadership positions have failed to provide you with their vision. Nevertheless, you know the purpose and mission of your company or department. From that, you can articulate the vision, and you should do that right away. Why? Because your vision for your project or team must support the larger vision.**

ATTITUDE 12

NURTURE JOY

... for the joy of the Lord is your strength.
Neh. 8:10 NASB

What does an attitude of joy have to do with being a leader with Christlike qualities? Who wants a project leader or team that spends time joking around or laughing? It is time-consuming and unprofessional. Projects are hard work. There is a deadline to meet.

Something in us should have rebelled at least a little bit as we read these statements, although we have all worked with clients and other volunteers in charity projects who feel this way. Some say they are paying a lot of money for quality results in a specified time, and there shouldn't be any fooling around on the clock. Some say they can't afford to give away time they don't have to join in unnecessary frivolity.

Adding Strength to Our Project

Working with our cohorts in an attitude of joy isn't the same as fooling around, telling jokes, or playing games. We express joy in the way we speak to people, in the way we approach our work assignment, and in the way we convey our respect for our supervisors, our associates, and our project itself.

What is joy? It is the emotion brought on when we experience a great happiness or pleasure ... when we experience something that brings us a special enjoyment. We experience joy with the success of a job well done. Joy is the emotion evoked by our feelings of well-being, success, or blessing. If we can convey the underlying tone and mood of joy to our team, the project will advance more quickly and with more team effort. Our team members will be more motivated and have a sense of well-being. They will feel fortunate to be working on the project and not feel as though they were sentenced to it, like a prisoner. They will feel they are doing a good thing, not only for themselves, their families, and their careers, but also for the common good of their teammates. They will feel blessed and that they are being a blessing to others.

How do we go about accomplishing this? There is no one method. Treating people well, caring for them as individuals, respecting their abilities to the point of gaining their agreement, and showing them an exciting vision and a means for its attainment will all serve to foster a sense of well-being. Joy is the result.

The Joyless Project

It is easy to spot the joyless project. The project team members feel like robots rather than people. They are reluctant to show their enthusiasm, even when they have some, for fear it will be exploited. They peer over their shoulders with apprehension and look ahead to the project's end. They find fault with it and behave negatively. Their moods are those of apathy, caution, irritation, frustration, apprehension, and boredom.

In terms of cause and effect, these are the effects. The cause of them is what is important. No amount of free lunches, happy hours, small cash bonuses, or pats on the back will change the situation or the attitudes of our team members. In fact, the law of sowing and reaping is in full force. Bad seeds have been planted, and it will take a season of better seed sowing to improve the harvest.

We leaders must aspire to have an attitude of joy in our projects. We must practice the attitudes of servanthood, the Sabbath, and a clear and worthwhile vision. If we do so from the first day the project begins, we will not only experience joy ourselves, but we will see and feel the joy grow in the work environment.

By demonstrating our own joy in the situation and our personal sense of well-being and feelings of good fortune at being associated with the project, we will, hopefully, inspire the same attitude in others. If we don't have this sense of joy, we must work toward acquiring it. We must find out why our attitude toward the project is so uncertain and make change our highest priority.

Dealing with the Joy Stealers

What are some things that can work against a joyful project? Perhaps our client refuses to go along with putting things in writing. Perhaps our own manager has not delivered a sufficient number of skilled persons to do the job in accordance with the schedule. Perhaps our manager doesn't possess even a few essential leadership skills. Perhaps we are taking over a troubled project mid-course, and it is clear that no positive attitudes are evident.

These are all difficult problems to overcome. Yet, they must be overcome ... for the sake of our own sanity, for the sake of our client's ultimate success, and for the sake of our team. This is where we really earn our paycheck as a manager, with the leadership qualities of Jesus.

The Joyful Project

The universal principles we have talked about are real and effective. We plant our seeds and expect a harvest of like kind. We practice the Golden Rule with everyone, no matter how anyone is treating us. We create a vision that is compelling for our entire team, our boss, and our client.

I can absolutely attest to the success of this method of leadership. I have yet to begin a project from the very beginning. I am always called in when the project is in trouble. Needless to say, joy is nonexistent on these projects.

Since I know the power behind a joyful work experience, I begin my leadership role by working on attitudes ... the project team's, the client's, my manager's, and my own. I lead from the front and take all the blame. I settle for nothing less than full agreement on everything. I treat everyone the way I would want to be treated. I craft a vision statement and map out a way to fulfill the vision. I build a longing to complete the vision in all parties. I replace those who simply cannot or will not see or accept the vision. I make certain everyone knows how important every little detail is to the overall success of our project.

Most of all, I reach the point where I believe that the project is the specific one I should be working on. It is worthy of my time and energy; it is a joyful way to spend my days. This is important because I must lead from the front, demonstrating with integrity my own beliefs about the project, the client, and the project team.

We must never underestimate the value, strength, and necessity of joy. It is a real force that provides great benefits and advantages to our projects. We must have a serious attitude toward joy. We must determine that it be present in good supply on every project, and when it isn't, we must realize that it is up to us to bring it about. Joylessness is a disease that will only grow until it destroys everything positive about our work.

We don't treat joylessness with parties, gifts, and a daily joke in our e-mail communications. Joy is not simply smiles or laughter. It goes much deeper. To create a sense of joy in the participants of a project, we must encourage a personal sense of well-being, good fortune, fulfillment, and success. We must instill a deep pleasure in participating in a job well done. We must assure that everyone involved experiences a sense of elation, euphoria, or excitement over each small achievement.

Only by adopting and adhering to the right attitudes—Christlike attitudes—can we cure our pessimistic project situation. As the appointed leader, we have it within our power to administer a miraculous cure. As a Christlike leader, we have an obligation to foster joy into our project team's day-to-day experiences.

ATTITUDE ALIGNMENT:

Will Your Attitude Be to Nurture Joy?

1. **Do you often have trouble being excited about your work?**
   - No one is excited about their job all the time. But are you finding it harder and harder to get excited at all?
2. **Do you think that your attitude can have a positive or negative impact upon those around you?**
   - If you are excited to be with the team, do you think they will see that? How about if you are dragging yourself through the motions? Will they see that, too?
3. **Do you believe that people accomplish more and with better quality when they are joyful?**
   - Don't you? When you are bored with the job, do you give it your all, all the time?
4. **This can be a difficult attitude for those who are not naturally optimistic and happy. Many successful leaders are naturally pragmatic or even melancholy. Still, the attitude is to nurture joy in yourself and others. The requirement is to recognize the power of joy and to seek it. What will that look like in your life? What will be different starting tomorrow?**

ATTITUDE 13

MIND THE SEASONS

While the earth remains, seedtime and harvest, cold and
heat, summer and winter, day and night, shall not cease.
Gen. 8:22 ESV

In today's non-agrarian, technological society, we no longer treat the changing of the seasons—or even recognize that there are seasons—with the same sense of wonder and reverence that our distant ancestors did. We have overcome the dictates of the weather. We purchase watermelons, strawberries, and tomatoes all year long at our local supermarkets because of easy access to imported products and sophisticated indoor nurseries. We can even sit in an outdoor 110-degree hot tub at the base of a ski slope while snowdrifts surround the deck and the thermometer reads twenty degrees Fahrenheit.

We may have overcome many attributes of the different seasons, but we have not prevented them from occurring year after year. Some of us believe the purpose behind a monolithic stone structure like Stonehenge was to provide a way to predict the arrival of the four seasons. Farmers want to know when it is safe to plant a crop. Plant too early in the spring, and a killing frost might wipe it out. Plant too late in the spring, and the crops may not have sufficient time to grow before a killing autumn frost.

Before the Stonehenge calendar, however, we had to figure out that there were seasons when certain things could not be accomplished and others when they could. We also had to figure out that these seasons came in a set sequence time after time after time. Many animals migrate with the seasons, some trees change dramatically with the seasons, oceans ebb and swell with seasonal regularity, and the position of the sun and stars appears to be dictated by the seasons.

Today, we understand more about these ancient truths than ever before, but we have yet to fully comprehend their influence on us and on our team members. We have yet to build our Stonehenge for projects because we have failed to pay attention to what is so obviously going on around us.

What Do Seasons Have to Do with Leadership?

Our lives are defined by seasons. In one season, we are children. In another season, we go to college to learn more about a particular subject of interest and to acquire skills that will enable us to support ourselves. In yet another season, we give birth to and raise children. In another, we prepare for retirement. Finally, we reach the season of retirement and enjoy more leisure activities and reflection, but we also have more concerns about our health.

While these seasons occur in most of our lives, some of us experience only a few because we must still deal with serious and often incurable diseases, increased traffic accidents, terrorist attacks on our cities, wars, and senseless murders. Each of these shortens the seasons of our lives or changes the quality of those we experience. We try juvenile offenders as adults in our courts. We push the retirement age higher as we live longer and healthier lives. We encourage our children to begin work projects at earlier ages. We extend the childbearing age of women through the use of new drugs and medical techniques. We encourage everyone to start a new career after retiring from the first one.

The relative virtues or disadvantages of these modern-day practices can be debated, but we ignore the seasons of our lives to our peril ... especially when they involve our management roles.

A Callous Disregard for the Obvious

If we are asked to manage a four-year project to build a new automated tax administration system (like I did at the IRS during the early 1990s), we must have a vision (probably several visions—one for each interim release of the system) and a master schedule. We must have a large team of people on and contiguous to the project. How does the law of the seasons help or hurt us?

Predicting the Future

Our chief system architect, Sally, is a professional thirty-five-year-old woman who has been married for ten years. She and her husband decide to start a family. Our project sponsor, Keith, is approaching his thirtieth year of service with the government and is eligible for early retirement. He plans to take it. Our product manager, Gary, is a great guy whose youngest child has recently graduated from college and married. Gary and his wife want to travel more and work less, something they have always wanted to do. My own father-in-law has been diagnosed with cancer, and my spouse is spending more time with him, leaving me with the care of our two teenagers. The funding for our project is dependent upon congressional approval on an annual basis. For the past several years, the Democrats have been in power, and the funding of our project was a high priority. The Republicans have just won the congressional majority.

Each of these situations is completely predictable for someone who is attuned to the law of the seasons. However, most reactive managers find themselves in trouble. "It was an unforeseen situation ... a real crisis!" "These sudden disruptions will be the death of my project!" "How can I be successful when so many impossible obstacles keep popping up?" "It's not my fault she got pregnant!"

As exceptional leaders who incorporate Christlike leadership qualities, we can do better. How can we justify an unanticipated delay in the schedule because a key team member announces she's *suddenly* taking maternity leave! How can we justify delays or unfinished work if our project sponsor retires unexpectedly? We can certainly understand when a sudden sickness occurs to a member of our team or to one of their family members, but it shouldn't be a surprise to us that it will happen to someone on our project team ... sooner or later.

It is more difficult for us to stay in sync with those who are changing from the mode of career building and advancement into career consolidation and ramp-down, as did the product manager, Gary, in the example. But, again, if we are involved in the lives of our team members, such matters are manageable events. We will not be surprised, and we will be prepared with a solution.

As quality leaders, we want to be aware of various seasonal concerns in the lives of those outside our immediate team, but we can't always predict the effect they might have on the members of our team. If we are a youth soccer coach and our star goalie, who will get our team into the finals, has a father who loses his job, we may not correctly manage our goalie if he doesn't confide in us. Only if we know about the situation can we make plans and take actions to mitigate the threat to our team. If our project involves the support of a congress-woman who faces a tough re-election fight, what will we do if she loses that fight? What steps should we take right now to lessen potential risk to our project?

Building Our Own Stonehenge

The aforementioned examples are all seasonally based episodes. As attentive leaders, if we are aware of the seasons in our team members' lives, they become manageable. We have essentially built our own Stonehenge. We know of the upcoming retirement of the project sponsor and have put into our project plan activities that will ease the project's transition to a new one. We know of the upcoming birth of Sally's baby and plan accordingly. We have a conversation with her about her maternity leave plans. We know whether she wants to return full-time or part-time and when. We also know that unforeseen things can occur, like a sudden illness in a project member's family. That is why we practice effective management techniques such as delegation and succession planning.

It is foolishness, if not management malpractice, to believe that everything will go as planned on a project, and if it doesn't, it isn't in any way our fault. The longer the project life cycle, the more foolish this notion is. The larger the project team, the more foolish it is. The more complex the project solution and/or technology, the more foolish we will appear for allowing these avoidable situations to interfere with the project's success.

As a quality leader/manager, it is our job to be aware of the seasons. They can be recognized, and their inherent risks can be mitigated. The farmer—and the manager—who ignores the seasons deserves to starve ... and usually does.

ATTITUDE ALIGNMENT:

Will Your Attitude Be to Mind the Seasons?

1. **Are you currently leading a multi-month project?**
   - Coaching a sports team? Supervising a nursing ward? Foreman of a construction crew? Dispatcher for a trucking company?
2. **Are you aware of what season the other people around you are in?**
   - Is anyone near retirement? Is anyone trying to have a child? Is anyone coming up on their sabbatical from work? Is anyone building a new house?
3. **What season of life you are in?**
   - What is about to change?
   - What is about to arrive and what is about to leave?
4. **Do you need additional career training? Do you have a child approaching 18 years old? Are your parents physically or financially healthy?**

ATTITUDE 14

BE VIGILANT

Be sober, be vigilant; because your adversary the devil, as a roaring lion, walketh about, seeking whom he may devour.
I Pet. 5:8 KJV

While a great many managers ignore or refuse to face realities, we will not. It is eminently possible for us to deal effectively, compassionately, and spiritually with many of the more severe problems that confront us. Whether we are leaders of a million-dollar software development project, softball coaches, Sunday school teachers, high school teachers, pastors, restaurant managers, shop foremen, company commanders, dispatchers, shift leaders, construction bosses, or new parents ... we can all perform our roles and responsibilities better if we incorporate the qualities and attitudes of Jesus Christ into the management of our projects. Our job is to adopt these attitudes so He might use us to better the lives of those whom we serve. When we do so, we take better care of our projects, our teammates, our clients, and ourselves.

This is truly a case of where the Scripture verse "He must increase, but I must decrease" (John 3:30 NASB) applies. The longer we keep our flawed attitudes, the longer we will plant defective seeds, destroy joy, disappoint our clients, frustrate our teammates, and experience failure. We must continuously strive to improve our attitudes and hold God's standard of perfection as our goal.

Things Will Still Go Wrong

In our religious lives, we talk of the flesh, evil, and the devil. In our secular lives, we speak of Murphy's Law. The truth is that no matter how much we love a summer of lying on the beach, we know a less pleasant time is coming. The very existence of summer foreshadows a not-so-comfortable winter season. The delights of daylight are preceded and followed by the gloominess of nighttime. These things will not change.

The lesson for us to learn is that no matter how much we prepare, no matter how many rules and truths we apply, no matter how talented our team members may be, sooner or later, bad things will happen.

The Cost of Vigilance

Every military commander knows he will suffer casualties on the battlefield. Some members of his team will be either wounded or killed. Despite this reality, he tries to lessen the inevitability. He makes careful and detailed plans; he trains his soldiers hard; he makes certain he has enough equipment and that it is in good condition; he assigns a medic to every platoon; he establishes medical evacuation teams and sets up field hospitals ... and, he makes sure the morale of his team members is kept high. Hope of survival is imperative for success of the project mission. The military commander cannot wait until he has casualties and then react with an ineffective and inadequate plan. He must know what his reaction will be for every expected action.

We are commanders of our team projects, and we must take the same precautions. Our teammates deserve it. It is not their job to do our work or shoulder our responsibility.

If we find that the "build phase" of our software project or our new church addition is progressing extremely well, we must fight the urge to become complacent and let down our guard. Easy success is not normal. We owe it to our client, our project, our teammates, and our boss to be concerned about the future. We must be vigilant.

Expect Trouble

Like the watchman in the tower of a castle, we leaders must remain vigilant against the dangers that threaten our teammates and projects. There are dangers everywhere. They are all around us. Therefore, more than anyone else, we must be on the lookout for them. If we are watchful enough, we will seldom be taken by surprise.

This truth can be joyfully liberating. Knowing that there will be continuing problems, we can more accurately set our expectations for the future. We can more accurately prepare our client and team for the inevitable. Then, having prepared them for the challenges ahead, they are not discouraged and dismayed when the mishaps occur. They take them in full stride. They welcome them as trials to be overcome. They take pride in being successful, despite the obstacles that seemed to slow them down or steal their possibility for success.

Some will call this attitude "worrying about nothing" or "making something out of nothing," but there is no indignity or chagrin from being a vigilant leader. Adopt the expression "Expect the worst, and you will never be disappointed."

This is not a pessimistic motto, but rather a liberating one. If we always expect the best from other people and life, then we will likely experience disappointment. Of course, we must assume that other people and life in general are good, but we also must expect things to go wrong. We need not worry about finding fault when it does. It is merely the way things are.

All of creation teaches us that in order for something to survive, something else must die. Field rats eat the farmer's grain, snakes eat the field rats, hawks eat the snakes (and the rats), and so forth. It is no different in the management world. There are some things out there that feed upon our projects. We must be forever vigilant against the hawks of our destruction. If we are project managers, we must be vigilant against team member turnover, against external dependencies upon which our team members depend for their own ability to succeed, and against changes in the requirements and wishes of our clients. If we are coaches, we must be vigilant against team member injuries. If we are truck dispatchers, we must be vigilant about weather and road conditions. If we are pastors, we must be vigilant against sin or the appearance of sin surrounding our ministry, against apathy in the pews, and against factions within the congregation. If we are department heads, we must be vigilant about securing and maintaining our operating budget, about retaining our highly trained team members, and about making concrete contributions to our corporation's bottom line. If we are parents, we must be vigilant about ... everything!

Forewarned Is Forearmed

The truth is that problems are beyond our frail power to either hinder or hurry. They strike all of us. All of the universe's vagaries teach us this is so. Things will continue to go wrong, no matter how well we plan or how alert we are. This is an important concept to learn. Therefore, as quality leaders, we will not be overly concerned when problems beset our projects. They are a normal happenstance on every project, no matter how large or small, trivial or important. It is our job to anticipate them before they happen and to mitigate their adverse impact upon our team members and the project itself. To do this, we will have procedures, policies, and contingency plans in place to quickly and effectively deal with each problem as it arrives. Is it easy to do? No. Do we have the option of not planning for the inevitable? No, we don't.

"Mr. Scott, We Need More Power!"

A spaceship orbits a planet. The ship is only able to maintain a stable orbit by applying an appropriate amount of force against the constant pull of the planet's gravity. If the spaceship lowers its guard, it will suffer the dire consequences of crashing into the surface of the planet.

There is a negative pull against us leaders at all times, and it requires that we take positive actions to overcome it. In the simplest of terms, if we don't eat and drink, we die. If we don't breathe, we die. If we don't plan, nothing is accomplished. If we don't set targets and make goals, nothing gets completed. This pull—like gravity—is not bad in and of itself. But like gravity, if we aren't vigilant against it, it will destroy us.

Therefore, we must take positive action. We must be proactive. We must be leaders who know there are casualties in every great endeavor. We must be resolute about minimizing these casualties. We must plant the right seeds and expect to harvest a productive crop. Feral fields do not produce corn crops. Starving cows yield no milk. Underattended projects spiral downward to their own destruction. We are the farmers, the generals, the starship captains of our projects, teams, churches, offices, groups, and clubs. As such, we are the servants of others. We must feed those we lead, plant good seeds and care for them attentively, and guard against the inevitable. If we do, we will be successful servants and leaders worthy of our calling.

In Closing

As we seek to become more Christlike in our leadership of others, we must contemplate and come to value the attitudes Jesus used in such positive and effective ways. And then we must work at emulating them every day until they become a natural part of our leadership style. If we do this and allow

Jesus Christ to lead others through us, we will enjoy more successes than failures and effectively finish projects with positive results.

It is unlikely that we will become perfect leaders, but it is worthwhile to aspire to that end. It is worth repeating that God does not require perfection from His children on Earth, but He encourages us to develop an attitude for it and to continuously put that attitude to work in our roles as leaders ... with His support. As a leader of mankind, Jesus possessed every positive attitude we could ever need and used them fruitfully and memorably. As Christlike leaders, we should continuously work to adopt these same attitudes into our lives.

Tend (nurture, guard, guide, and fold) the flock of God that is [your responsibility], not by coercion or constraint, but willingly; not dishonorably motivated by the advantages and profits [belonging to the office], but eagerly and cheerfully; Not domineering [as arrogant, dictatorial, and overbearing persons] over those in your charge, but being examples (patterns and models of Christian living) to the flock (the congregation).
I Pet. 5:2, 3 The Amplified Bible

ATTITUDE ALIGNMENT:

Will Your Attitude Be to Be Vigilant?

1. **Recall a time when you were negatively surprised by something that happened.**
   - Was it fun? Would you like to avoid these surprises in the future?

2. **Do your current plans reflect a best case scenario rather than a most likely case?**
   - Is that reasonable? How many major changes have you already made, or should have made, to your plans?
   - Do you consider surprises unavoidable no matter what you do?
   - Do you think that always looking for bad things to happen causes bad things to happen?

3. **Being vigilant can look to others like you are a pessimist with no joy, no vision, and no plan. And yet, having a plan, a vision, and joy does not replace the need for vigilance. What to do? Embrace it all ... all of the attitudes. What will joyful, passionate, visionary, vigilant leadership look like in your life?**

FINAL ATTITUDE CHECK

So, how did you do? As you scored your current attitudes and actions, did you like what you saw? Was there room for improvement on only a few attitudes, or do you need to do better on nearly all of them?

That is to be expected. To be perfect is our attitude, our intention, even our ultimate goal ... but we will never actually achieve it. Fortunately, we do not need to. The consistent adoption of these attitudes is enough for now. With God's help, it is sufficient. The spiritual laws behind them work every time, for everyone. Just do your best to be faithful in these important ways and leave the rest up to God. And to do that, may I also suggest that you start each day with a prayer?

Dear Lord,

Again, today, I need you.
Help me to serve others.
Guide me as I lead others.
Protect me while I care for others.
Forgive me when I fail.
Strengthen me where I am weak.
Let no harm come to those around me.
May they see You in me and be blessed.
I want to be more like Jesus.

Amen.

About William C. Oakes, PMP

After high school, Bill enlisted in the U.S. Army in the early 1970s. He served for eleven years as a Vietnamese and Russian translator.

Upon leaving the military, Bill started a career in computer programming, consulting, training, and project management. He has worked for companies such as Oracle, Sybase, Martin Marietta, and the Internal Revenue Service. He has served clients such as the U.S. Air Force, the U.S. Navy, the U.S. Air Force Academy, the Internal Revenue Service, NASA, and the U.S. Department of the Interior.

Today, Bill is a practicing project management professional and instructor, as well as an ordained minister and author. He still practices and encourages others to adopt the Christlike attitudes taught in this book through his website and blog at www.william-oakes.com.

.

www.ingramcontent.com/pod-product-compliance
Lightning Source LLC
LaVergne TN
LVHW051416080426
835508LV00022B/3107